THE MAGNIFICENT ADVENTURES OF ALEXANDER MACKENZIE

Noel B. Gerson

SAPERE BOOKS

THE
MAGNIFICENT
ADVENTURES OF
ALEXANDER
MACKENZIE

Published by Sapere Books.

20 Windermere Drive, Leeds, England, LS17 7UZ,
United Kingdom

saperebooks.com

ISBN: 978-1-80055-393-4.

TABLE OF CONTENTS

I: THE ICY FURNACE   6

II: THE MAKING OF AN EXPLORER   13

III: THE APPRENTICE   20

IV: PRELUDE TO ADVENTURE   36

V: THE RIVER AND THE MOUNTAINS   48

VI: DANGERS IN THE ARCTIC   61

VII: THE GRIM VOYAGE   71

VIII: THE HOMECOMING   82

IX: GOLD AND GLORY: PREPARATION FOR ADVENTURE   91

X: THE GREAT ADVENTURE   103

XI: THE WILDERNESS ROAD   116

XII: ACROSS THE GREAT DIVIDE   126

XIII: CATASTROPHE ON THE BAD RIVER   137

XIV: DIPLOMAT IN BUCKSKINS   147

XV: THE NORTHWEST PASSAGE   157

XVI: THE LAND OF PLENTY   166

XVII: THE PACIFIC OCEAN   176

XVIII: SURVIVAL OF THE STRONG   187

XIX: THE LAST MARCH   197

AFTERMATH   206

SELECTED BIBLIOGRAPHY   213

A NOTE TO THE READER   215

I: THE ICY FURNACE

A HOWLING WIND roared down the snow-covered slopes of the towering mountains, bending the trunks of pine trees. The sky overhead was dark and ominous clouds obscured the summits of the great peaks. This sky, in the unknown, uncharted, and untamed wilderness of the Continental Divide in western Canada, was called "the lid of the Universe." Alexander Mackenzie gave it that name.

A few flakes of snow were driven down by the wind. Then, all at once, the great cauldron of the "Universe" seemed to tip. The air was filled with ice and snow — stinging pellets that burned men's faces, lodged in their clothes, and made them wish they had not abandoned the comfortable hearths, snug log cabins, and food-filled warehouses back east.

At the timber line one man stood alone. A vast sea of trees spread out below him, a rubble of rocks and boulders above. Young, still in his twenties, he was very short, with small bones, a slender build, and the delicate features of a poet. His face, however, was gaunt now after long weeks in the wilderness. The sun and wind had darkened his skin, a week's stubble covered his chin and his buckskins were worn and ripped. But holding his head high, he shook his fist at the elements. Then he laughed, a full-throated, hearty laugh of genuine pleasure.

The men who huddled behind him were not surprised, for they knew that Alexander Mackenzie was possessed by demons. There was no other explanation for his inexhaustible energy, his coldly calculated daring. Nor could the men who accompanied him, in the spring and summer of 1792, on his journey of exploration to find the overland, northwest passage across the North American continent to the Pacific Ocean, understand his insatiable curiosity, his lack of fear, and, above all, his ability to drive others as he drove himself.

His Indian guides were certain that creatures from the netherworld had occupied his body and soul. Each night they prayed to their gods of fire and water, sun and earth and sky, in the forlorn hope that he would turn back. His *voyageurs*, hard-muscled and hard-headed French-Canadians, boasted that their physical strength was unequaled in all the world. Now, however, they had more than met their match. For even though they often paddled their canoes or bateaux eighteen hours a day and marched all day and most of the night across wilderness portages, they needed at least a few hours of rest in each twenty-four. Mackenzie, apparently, needed none at all.

Henry Fuller Bishop of New Haven, Connecticut, a youth of twenty-one, had accompanied Mackenzie on his previous journey of exploration three years earlier. He should not have been surprised by his leader's behavior. But even Bishop was dazed by Mackenzie's fury. Alexander Mackay, the second-in-command of the expedition and Mackenzie's Scottish compatriot, was a man of good education, blessed with a strong body and a mind and will of his own. But he, too, had lost his individual identity somewhere in the trackless wilderness of plains and hills, deep forests and swift-flowing rivers. His mind was numbed, his legs and arms ached ceaselessly, yet he still responded to the goading of the short, slender man with the flashing eyes and the deep voice who sometimes pleaded and begged, sometimes roared and thundered.

Everyone knew that the Pacific lay somewhere to the west, Mackenzie insisted. And he was determined to find the passage that would take him to its shores, no matter how great the obstacles. Hostile Indians could not halt him. Mackenzie even refused to quit when his guides admitted they were lost. Neither burning heat nor bone-chilling cold slowed his pace.

Had Alexander Mackenzie been a giant, the men might have found it easier to believe in him, to follow him blindly. But he was only five feet, five inches tall; his wrists, waist, and ankles were as slim as a girl's. To see him in action was frightening. Arousing his companions at two or three o'clock in the morning, he hurried them through breakfast, then broke trail. Accompanied by guides, he marched all day with two ninety-pound packs of life-sustaining pemmican slung across his narrow shoulders, a small arsenal of weapons jammed into his belt, his telescope and other scientific instruments on his back, and his precious notebooks filling his pockets.

Mackenzie walked bareheaded, exposing himself to torrential rains and the merciless rays of the sun. His hair was long and shaggy, his skin as dark and leathery as that of the natives; his buckskins were worn thin. Whenever the party stopped for a brief meal and rest, he wrote in his notebooks about birds, animals, and plants they had encountered, and described the territory they had covered.

When the *voyageurs* faltered, he helped them carry their heavily laden boats. When the Indians fell ill, he boiled herbs and cured them. When young Bishop became melancholy, he told robust jokes that made the boy laugh. Sometimes he marched at Bishop's side and, although only twenty-nine years of age himself, spoke with such mature wisdom that he might have been Bishop's father. When Mackay argued that they were bound on a fool's errand and surely would die, he replied with a stubborn logic of his own: the Pacific was somewhere to the west; they had wits and ability; so they were sure to reach their goal if they kept on.

At night, when the others were rolled up in their blankets and fast asleep, he studied the stars through his telescope. Then, working on his maps by the fight of the campfire, he carefully charted their position. Then he labored some more on his notebooks. The Indians, who sometimes awoke in the night, swore that he never slept. Perhaps they exaggerated, but he was certainly refreshed after remarkably short periods of rest.

Now, after grueling weeks of travel up rushing rivers and portages where boiling rapids made progress by boat impossible, the party faced its most severe test. Mackenzie was leading them, on foot, to the very roof of the world! They toiled up the slopes of mountains, each higher and more rugged than the one behind it. They plunged into tiny, narrow valleys, then resumed their climb toward peaks covered with pure, white snow. The men staggered beneath their loads, sweat oozed from their pores; they were forced to pause every few minutes to catch their breath. But Mackenzie remained cheerful, smiling when they groaned, encouraging them with a few gentle words when they wept.

Mackay felt certain they were crossing territory never before seen by man. Mackenzie scoffed at the idea. And one afternoon, as the party emerged from a forest of pines and headed toward the timberline of a rugged peak, loud war whoops broke the silence. Indian braves were lurking behind the screen of trees; their hail of arrows forced the explorers to take shelter.

Mackenzie promptly advanced toward the natives, calling to them first in one dialect, then in another. There was no response, so he called again, swearing that he and his companions had peaceful intentions toward all men.

An arrow cut through the leather of his stained buckskins. Mackenzie drew a pistol, but deliberately fired it into the air. The shot echoed and re-echoed across the mountains. The braves, cowed by this display of might, emerged into the open. Mackenzie then opened a pack containing trading goods and presented each of the five braves with a knife. To their leader he gave an iron cooking-pot, a string of beads, and a burnished square of steel that could be used as a mirror.

Now the other explorers left the shelter of boulders. The two parties sat down together over a fire, the natives willingly sharing their fish and jerked elk meat. The *voyageurs* and guides ate ravenously as did Mackay and Bishop. But Alexander Mackenzie was indifferent to food; he wanted information.

He failed to get it. The braves said they had never reached the crest of the mountain range and doubted that anyone could climb that high. If the strangers went higher, they would find no wild life because there were no forests. The headwaters of rivers churned too rapidly for even the hardiest of fish to survive. There were no plants, no edible roots on the heights where snow lay deep throughout the year. And the natives were reluctant to explain other, mysterious terrors.

Mackenzie, brushing aside their superstitions, persisted in his questioning. Had they ever met men who had actually crossed the mountains? Had they even heard of anyone who had performed such a feat?

The Indians reluctantly admitted that, many years in the past, three warriors from a strange tribe had suddenly appeared in the highlands, saying that they lived on the far side of the mountains.

Did they resemble other Indians?

No, the braves said, they were taller, huskier, and their skins were paler.

Mackenzie had learned what he wanted most to know: the mountain range could be conquered. He stood apart, his face impassive. No one knew he was finding it difficult to curb his mounting sense of excitement. Soon now he must test the theory on which he was staking the lives of his followers as well as his own.

His thoughts must have turned back to the long winter of 1786-87 which he spent with Peter Pond, his good friend and mentor, in a trading post hut on the Athabaska River. There the grizzled veteran who had explored so much of the northwest had chatted for hours with the young man destined to excel him. Together they had developed a new concept of the geography of the North American continent.

Both knew that a high range of mountains, running north and south, cut them off from the Pacific; they called this range the Great Divide. Apparently the rivers running down the eastern slopes of these mountains all flowed toward the east. They had learned this from personal observation and from questioning natives who had penetrated deeper into the chain of massive peaks.

So the rivers on the far side of this chain must flow toward the west. If their theory was right, these streams emptied into the Pacific Ocean.

Common sense dictated that the idea was correct. But Mackenzie was no longer a neophyte. He had already gained lasting renown on an earlier journey of discovery. And he had found repeatedly that Nature confounded the logic of mere mortals. So he would not believe that the Pacific was somewhere ahead until he saw with his own eyes that the rivers past the summit flowed westward.

And what if he were wrong? Well, in that case he had no guidelines. With luck, he and his party might reach the shores of the world's largest sea. But they also might wander through the maze of mountains until they froze or starved to death.

He had no idea when, if ever, the party would eat another hot meal. He didn't know whether they would find their way out of the snow-glazed morass at the top of the world. But there was only one way to go — forward...

II: THE MAKING OF AN EXPLORER

LIFE IN THE HEBRIDES, a group of some five hundred islands that lies off the west coast of Scotland, was bleak in the last quarter of the eighteenth century. But it offered challenges, too, and Alexander Mackenzie, born in 1763 or 1764 and now in his teens, was a courageous youngster.

Most of the men and women who lived in the little port town of Stornoway on the east coast of the island of Lewis worked hard to earn a precarious living; they had little interest in the outside world. At this time the great and powerful Hudson's Bay Company was completing its first century of operations in Canada and was sending home a seemingly unending flow of furs to the Old World. This caused an occasional comment, but only because a few courageous men from the Hebrides had set themselves up in Montreal as independent fur traders and, daring to fight "The Company" as it was always called, were earning large fortunes.

Poverty-stricken Stornoway was fascinated by wealth. Most of her citizens earned a bare living by fishing for herring; others raised cattle and sheep on the rocky hillsides where grass was scarce. The town boasted two churches, one school, and an old abandoned castle. According to legend, the Mackenzies of Seaforth, as Alexanders family was called, had once been the lords of Lewis. Now, however, the boy's father was as poor as everyone else.

Alexander lived in a small stone hut with his parents; he was their only child. He attended school for just five or six years, the maximum period then available, but unlike the other children of Stornoway, he was not content to stop learning after his formal education ceased. Small and sickly, he had often succumbed to severe head colds and could not take part in rough, childish games. Instead, he had spent much of his time reading. Neighbors, knowing he had memorized long passages from the King James Bible, predicted that Alexander would become a clergyman.

The family's minister, Pastor MacVeigh of the Church of Scotland, encouraged the lad. After Alexander completed his schooling, he was a frequent visitor to the MacVeigh house. There he borrowed many books from the clergyman's library, and was so quick-witted that he rapidly absorbed everything he read.

An eagerness for learning appeared to be a family trait, for, although Alexander was bright, he was considered less brilliant than his favorite cousin, Roderic Mackenzie, a year or two his junior. Early in life Roderic displayed a remarkable writing talent and Alexander was proud of his cousin's ability. All he himself could do, Alexander said, was to add a column of figures rapidly.

Alexander was, in fact, overly modest. He could do many things, and when he reached his teens, he proved himself the equal of any adult. Perhaps he was compensating for his short stature, slender build, and the years of illness that had made him a physical weakling. Whatever his reasons, he more than caught up with his contemporaries.

He went to sea regularly in the fishing boats and became expert at handling sails and oars, herring nets and the lines used to catch larger fish. Particularly enjoying rough weather, he liked to stand in the bow of a boat when huge waves smashed over her prow, drenching him. Many of Stornoway's fishermen had never learned to swim in the chilly waters, but

Alexander taught himself when he was twelve or thirteen. Soon he could swim farther than anyone he knew.

At home, as well as on the rocky cliffs leading down to the stormy sea, he proved himself unusually agile and surefooted. A slip, a loss of balance, or an unexpected misstep meant death in the churning waves that smashed below the rocks. Some neighbors thought Alexander odd because he spent so much time by himself on the cliffs. Often he could be seen sitting there, staring out at the sea and brooding.

There are high hills in the Hebrides, too. Alexander climbed to the peaks of many of them. When told that he was wasting his time, he merely shrugged and smiled. He allowed no one to dictate to him, and he was always at home in the outdoors in any kind of weather.

Certainly the climate in the Hebrides was far from ideal. But Alexander endured the dampness and the chill of winter without complaint. Only on the bitterest days would he consent to wear a greatcoat, stocking cap, and muffler, for he was determined to harden himself. After he passed his thirteenth birthday, he never again suffered from a head cold.

Residents of Stornoway who had visited Glasgow or Edinburgh thought their local diet monotonous and dull, but Alexander, who had gone twice to those cities with his parents, actually liked the home-town food. He ate herring and roast lamb and on special occasions sat down to a rump steak. His palate became accustomed to a lack of vegetables, too, for only potatoes, turnips, and a few other root plants grew in the rocky soil of Lewis. Believing it important to eat whatever was available, he had no interest in table delicacies.

As a boy, Alexander saw Nature in her most violent moods and was never frightened. He laughed at gales, blizzards, and tidal waves. He was also fascinated by all outdoor living things.

A tiny violet flower, growing in moss on a sun-warmed spot behind a sheltering rock, was an object to be identified — and cherished. A strange little crustacean washed up on the shore by a hostile sea was something to be studied with care. And the animals that roamed, singly or in packs, on the scores of uninhabited islands of the Hebrides were creatures to be accepted without fear, then mastered.

An incident that occurred when he was twelve years old was important in shaping his later life. The boys of Stornoway were forbidden to play on the rocks beyond a sharp point of land that jutted out into the open sea. Some of these boulders were huge. Anybody could walk out to them at low tide, but when the water rolled in, huge waves broke over the rocks, and a vicious cross-current made it dangerous for even the best athlete to try to swim to shore. Because several adolescents had lost their lives on those boulders, the people of Stornoway believed that the ghosts of the drowned boys haunted the area.

Alexander, however, could not resist the challenge. Late one afternoon in early autumn, he slipped away from his friends, went down to the point of land, and looked out at the boulders. The tide was just beginning to come in. If he hurried, he would have just enough time to race out to the farthest rock, then dash back to shore. Removing his boots and stockings, he started to run.

The water rose rapidly higher and higher. Soon he realized that he had miscalculated. Climbing onto the largest of the boulders, he scrambled to the top. In a few minutes the rock was surrounded by angry, churning foam. Waves dashed against the stone, drenching the boy in cold, salty spray.

Alexander clung to the summit, his fingers digging into crevices of the hard granite. A great breaker, smashing against the rock, rolled over him. Then came another and a third that almost washed him away. He gasped for breath, pressing close to the boulder. The nightmare seemed endless. Losing all count of the waves that crashed against the stone, he knew that, if he relaxed his vigilance for a single instant, he would drown.

When night came, a cold wind blew down from the high hills of the island. The boy's hands and feet became numb. Whenever he dared, he flexed his fingers for a moment or two, wiggled his toes, and pumped his legs in the air. Gradually the fury of the waves subsided. At last he found he could stand up. Exercising vigorously, he slipped and almost fell into the menacingly black water now swirling around the boulder.

Alexander took stock of his situation. He could not swim ashore; the sea was too deep, the unseen cross-currents below the rippling surface too strong. If only he was patient, he would survive. So he sat down and kept himself busy rubbing his chilled hands and arms, legs, and feet. Suddenly realizing he was hungry, he craved a steaming dish of oatmeal. But he sternly repressed all thoughts of food.

The worst of the danger was past; several hours, however, must elapse before the sea would retreat. Sensibly deciding to take a nap, he fell fast asleep in a few moments.

A party of fishermen set out after midnight to search for his body. The lights of their blazing torches revealed the boy calmly sleeping on top of the boulder. The fear in the faces of the men astonished Alexander. No one would believe him when he said he had enjoyed himself enormously.

At the age of thirteen, he conceived the idea of tabulating all the animal and plant life in the Hebrides. Two years later he actually completed the work. Roderic helped him to rewrite it, and Pastor McVeigh sent the pamphlet to Edinburgh. No publisher there proved interested, so the manuscript was forwarded to London where it met the same fate. Many years later, publishers gladly would have paid any amount of money for the privilege of printing the document, but by that time Mackenzie, always the perfectionist, had found it woefully incomplete and preferred to put it away in his private files.

Astronomy was another subject that caught young Alexander's attention. Like all seafarers, he had learned to chart his position at sea by the stars. But such calculations were rough, and when he found a book of astronomy in Pastor MacVeigh's library, he was fascinated. Then, buying his first, inexpensive telescope with money saved from his fisherman's pay, he amused himself on clear nights by going up to the hills outside Stornoway to study the skies.

By 1779, when Alexander was sixteen, Lewis and the Hebrides had grown too small for him. His mother had died and his father had remarried, and the boy felt ill at ease in his father's house. He could, of course, have moved elsewhere in the islands, but his imagination was captured by the tales of great wealth accumulated by Hebrides men who had migrated to Canada to enter the fur trade.

Alexander had had his fill of grinding poverty, of a barren existence eked out in herring fishing. There were only two alternatives if he remained at home. He could raise sheep, which did not appeal to him, or he could enter the ministry provided that he went back to school. He was not prepared to become a clergyman, he told Pastor MacVeigh. The minister sympathized with him, and he listened to the lad talk by the hour about going to the New World.

Then Alexander also discussed the idea at length with Roderic. The two boys made a pact. Alexander would go to Montreal, and after he had established himself there, Roderic would follow on his own sixteenth birthday. After coming to this decision, Alexander did not waste time in idle dreaming. After obtaining his father's permission to leave home, he took his savings — amounting to a few pieces of silver, and went to Glasgow.

There he finally found work, and signed an agreement to act as a ship's hand in return for his passage to Montreal. A few days later, his funds exhausted, he sailed as an ordinary seaman on a merchantman, a square-rigged brig with two masts. It was the first time in his life he had ever been aboard such a large vessel.

III: THE APPRENTICE

THE BOY WHO STOOD on the deck of the brig stared in wonder at the New World as the ship sailed slowly from Quebec to Montreal. Life in the Hebrides had been rugged, but the people there thought and spoke in terms of miles or, at the most, tens of miles. Now Alexander Mackenzie overheard Canadians talking casually about journeys of many hundreds of miles. Their nonchalance dumfounded the young emigrant.

He was dazed, too, by the huge expanses of forest. The cities of Quebec and Montreal were reputed to be civilized; so were the towns that dotted the banks of the mighty St. Lawrence between the two major centers. Yet the wilderness was everywhere. In the Hebrides, trees were carefully nurtured, but here, as far as the eye could see, were hundreds of thousands of maples and oaks, pines and silver birch.

Canada had remained loyal to the Crown after the thirteen colonies south of her border had declared their independence, so when Alexander arrived at Montreal in the autumn of 1779, he expected to find himself in an English-speaking land. He was bewildered to hear the vast majority of the city's residents speaking French. Only occasionally did his ears catch a welcome Scottish burr. He became all the more confused when someone told him that the citizens were wearing mourning to commemorate the nineteenth anniversary of France's surrender of Canada to Great Britain. And he was shocked to learn that garrisons in the city and the nearby village of Lachine had been strengthened to forestall possible pro-French demonstrations.

Montreal, with a population of ten thousand persons, was one of the New World's largest cities. The penniless newcomer, strolling down the St. Lawrence River waterfront, was impressed by the cavernous, closely guarded warehouses loaded with priceless furs from the west. There were taverns everywhere, most of them filled with raucous *voyageurs*, men who made the boy from the Hebrides wonder if he had landed on a continent of giants.

The *voyageurs* were unique. Most were French-Canadians, some were mixed-race. Their company numbered adventurers from a score of lands, among them England and the new United States. Without exception, the buckskin-clad *voyageurs* were tall, hard-muscled and lean. They earned their living as boatmen, paddling canoes, or tapering flat-bottomed bateaux that carried trading goods to the Indians in the west and returned loaded with furs. Accustomed to harsh discipline, incredibly long working hours, and careers forcing them to spend most of their lives in the wilderness, the *voyageurs* were, in the main, young. Hard, physical labor, a constant diet of meat and fish, and the risks of their trade killed them early in life. Then, too, when they came to Montreal to spend many months' wages in a few days, they often engaged in fatal brawls. Alexander gaped when he saw at least a dozen street fights that the constables did not even bother to halt.

The belligerent canoemen rarely stayed in the city for more than a few weeks at a time. They spent their money quickly, then vanished again into the wilderness of rivers and lakes and forests. North and west of the city were millions of acres of timberland. No one knew how far they extended, because few men had ever ventured beyond Grand Portage, the great trading post at the western end of Lake Superior, south of Lake Winnipeg.

Alexanders pockets were empty now. He carried all his worldly possessions in a sack slung over his shoulder. Redcoat recruiting sergeants tried to halt him, but he brushed past them hastily. He was interested in commerce, not politics. Alexander had come to Canada to earn a comfortable living; he did not intend to let either military campaigns or political upheavals deter him.

After wandering through the streets, he found himself in front of the two-story log building housing the offices of Gregory and MacLeod, a firm of prosperous Scottish merchants grown wealthy in the fur trade. Alexander went inside and asked to see the partners.

They interviewed him, heard the burr in his voice, and were impressed by his single-mindedness. He was hired on the spot as a junior clerk at a salary of three pounds, ten shillings per month.

Alexander found lodgings at a boarding house on St. Paul Street, one of Montreal's principal thoroughfares. Promptly at seven o'clock the next morning, he reported for work. He soon proved to be the most industrious of the company's employees. Certainly the lad seemed destined to live the rest of his life behind a desk, for he spent the next six years in that office. Roderic joined him there in 1781.

During those six years as a clerk, he traveled no farther from Montreal than Lachine where Gregory and MacLeod had warehouses. His muscles became flabby and he developed a slight paunch, but he absorbed a vast knowledge of fur trading. Above all, he became immersed in the merciless battle between "The Company" and the "pedlars."

The Company, of course, was the monolithic giant, the Hudson's Bay Company, founded a century earlier, after the restoration of Charles II, by the King's peripatetic cousin,

Prince Rupert. Ever since that time, The Company had dominated Canada's economy, regardless of whether she owed her allegiance to France or to England. Countless merchant ships had carried the furs of the Canadian wilderness to England and to Europe.

Now The Company's monopoly was being seriously threatened by men contemptuously called "pedlars." They were independent merchants with headquarters in Montreal. Their operatives in the field, traders who had opened new territories west and north of The Company's realm, were now making them rich and powerful. Gregory and MacLeod was such a concern, and in 1784 the meticulous, hard-working Alexander Mackenzie became one of its leading, though still junior, partners.

The fur trade, as he had learned, was a complicated industry. Goods purchased in England were transported to Montreal at considerable cost. These items, including rum, wine, gunpowder, shot, muskets, iron cooking utensils, and household goods, were unloaded in Montreal and repacked in bales weighing ninety pounds each. These bales or "pieces" were small and light enough to be handled with relative ease by a man traveling through the wilderness.

The pieces were loaded in canoes and bateaux at Montreal, and a trader, usually a partner or a senior clerk in one of the independent companies, was in charge of each trading venture. *Voyageurs* supplied the manpower.

Goods were transported via the St. Lawrence River and the Great Lakes into Indian country, the members of an expedition traveling on water when possible, on land when necessary. Dotted about the vast, trackless forests and plains were tiny trading posts, some staffed by only one man. At these stations supplies from Europe were traded for the

Indians' skins of beaver and otter, fox and lynx. Mackenzie estimated that one bateau loaded with trading goods was worth, by the time it reached the Indians, more than seven hundred pounds sterling. But, when a boat returned to Montreal, it carried furs valued at ten times that sum.

Early in 1785, the firm of Gregory and MacLeod expanded, taking in several new senior partners. One of them was the twenty-two-year-old Alexander Mackenzie, the outdoorsman who had been chained to a desk for six long years.

The New World was a continent of the young; it was not unusual for a youth to be made a *bourgeois* — or partner — in one of the major independent companies. Rarely, however, did someone with Alexander's lack of experience in the field become a senior executive. Eager to remedy that situation, he planned to lead an expedition in person. But his departure was delayed by a business merger of monumental importance in which he himself was a prime mover.

The pedlars had discovered that The Company's maneuvers were hurting them. Several young businessmen, including Alexander, decided to meet fire with fire by uniting. Some of the older executives were unable to agree with one another, so at first two new companies were formed. But as each realized that a merger would make them stronger, they set up the North-West Company in which all the leading pedlars of Montreal owned shares.

The deal concluded, Alexander announced that he intended to lead an expedition on a short trip to Fort Detroit. He still had a few lessons to learn, however, about the ways of New World society. For when he arrived at Lachine to start his journey, the *voyageurs* assigned to accompany him made no move to pack the boats with provisions and trading supplies. Instead, they stared impudently at the short, slender youth.

Unimpressed by his partnership, they began to discuss him as though he was not present and ended by insulting him roundly.

Alexander knew he would be forced to return to his office and stay there if he could not command even the respect of his boatmen. So, walking up to the tallest and burliest of the *voyageurs* known as "the Bear," he calmly challenged him to a fist fight.

The Bear stared at Alexander in amazement. Then suddenly lashing out, he sent the youngster sprawling with a single, vicious punch. The others roared with laughter as Alexander stood up and brushed himself off. But their laughter died away when he threw himself at the huge *voyageur*, his fists flailing. The Bear dropped to the ground, and the men blinked.

Then the *voyageur* hauled himself erect again. He lunged at his diminutive opponent, cursing fluently, but went down a second time. The fight went on for more than a quarter of an hour, only ending when the heavy-set canoeman had been knocked unconscious.

Alexander filled a pail with river water, dumped it over the man's head, and coolly ordered the boats packed at once. Two hours later the party shoved off. The Bear, now Alexander's staunch supporter, demanded and received the honor of acting as steersman in the leader's boat.

When Alexander's bateau left civilization behind, he smelled the clean odors of earth and trees, felt cool, rushing water beneath his head, and realized how much he had missed all this during the years spent in the city. He had come home — into his own.

The trading venture was moderately successful, but money alone no longer absorbed Alexander. He made up his mind to spend more time in the field. And at that turning point in his life, he became closely associated with Peter Pond, a trader and explorer whom the partners of the North-West Company had elected to the rank of *bourgeois*.

Had there been no Peter Pond, Alexander Mackenzie might have lived and died in obscurity. Instead, Pond inspired his protege and passed on to the younger man his precious dreams.

Pond, an iconoclast and rebel, a visionary and nonconformist, was a precursor of the nineteenth century Mountain Men famous in the legends of the American West. He was a "loner," an explorer who spent months and sometimes years making his way through vast areas that no other civilized man had ever seen. Pond was a scientist as well, though but a semi-literate. He kept maps and journals that helped those who came after him. Pond was a shrewd fur trader, a sharp businessman, and, to put it charitably, an eccentric. Above all, he was the man who searched unceasingly for the northwest passage to the Pacific.

Pond was justifiably feared throughout the northwest, for his temper was violent; he never hesitated to kill anyone standing in his path. A native of Milford, Connecticut, raised in dire poverty, he had gone to Canada in 1760 as a member of the military expedition that captured Montreal. He remained in the north country, became a *voyageur* for a few years, and then set out on his own as a trader. Far more than any other one man, Pond was responsible for opening to the fur trade the huge territory north and west of Lake Superior.

The fateful meeting of Mackenzie and Pond took place in the main hall of the log fort at Detroit. Alexander was sitting alone, quietly eating his supper, when the silence was shattered by loud shouting and the barking of dogs. He reached for his rifle which he had laid on the bench beside him, but the clerks sitting at other tables merely smiled apprehensively.

A moment later Pond stalked into the hall, a pack of dogs at his heels. The gray-haired giant had not shaved in weeks, his buckskins were stained, and he was badly in need of a bath. But his natural dignity was overwhelming. As he joined Alexander at the table reserved for partners in North-West, they felt an immediate sense of rapport. Pond ate a large venison steak, a platter of bear bacon, and a moose liver, and insisted that his dogs be given chunks of fresh meat, too. Alexander had finished his own meal, but he lingered on at the table.

Later in the evening, he and Pond wandered out into the open. They sat down together beneath a giant oak and talked until dawn. That is, Pond talked and Alexander listened as the older man expounded his theories of the geography of North America. If one sailed north up the Peace River from Lake Athabaska in what subsequently became the northern part of the Province of Alberta, one would travel through Unalaska to Kamchatka and eventually would reach England by way of Russia. Pond hoped to prove some day that his theory was accurate.

Of far greater importance to him, however, was his belief that the northwest passage to the Pacific could be found by journeying across the towering mountain range and finding rivers that drained toward the west.

Mackenzie listened with the greatest of respect, for Peter Pond was no foolish amateur. He was the discoverer of the Methye Portage, the line of demarcation separating waters that drain into Hudson's Bay from those that flow north. Following a small stream that had led him to the mighty Athabaska River which flows in a north-south line through the heart of Alberta, he had established a new trading post that had been the most successful in all history. Chipewyan and Cree Indians, who formerly had carried their furs to the far distant Hudson's Bay Company post at Churchill in what became the Province of Manitoba, now brought their skins instead to Pond's headquarters. The territory thus opened was too large for one man to handle alone, so Pond had accepted a partnership in North-West. As he explained to Alexander, a string of forts in the territory must be established and, equally important, food-storage huts must be built at strategic locations.

Alexander memorized Pond's every word, for he knew that this was the man who had pried from the natives the secret of how to survive long marches through barren wilderness. Pond was the first civilized human being to make and eat pemmican — sun-dried buffalo meat mixed with buffalo grease. Pemmican kept for long periods without spoiling.

The two men also discussed strange rumors both of them had heard. According to one such tale, Imperial Russia had set up permanent posts on the northern Pacific shores and was reaping a rich harvest in seal and otter. Alexander became excited; he told the older man of an account, published in London, about the last voyage of discovery made by the late Captain James Cook. Cook had explored and charted vast stretches of the coastline of the Pacific northwest. It was probable, Alexander thought, that the Russians had profited from the captain's journal.

In any event, Alexander and Pond agreed an overland route to the Pacific must be found in the next few years before others came along, discovered it, and reaped the profits.

Pond suspected that the Peace River emptied into the Pacific. He based the assumption on tales told him by Indians at his remote trading post. They swore they had actually visited the settlements of the Russians. But Pond couldn't be certain, for through the years he had learned that natives were facile liars. They often told the bearers of rum and firearms what those foreigners were anxious to hear. But no matter whether the stories were true, as Pond hoped, or false, as he feared, he was certain there must be an overland route to the Pacific.

He was determined to find it, then stake out the territory for North-West. In doing so, he would beat the sea captains of many nations hoping to discover along the coast a large river that emptied into the ocean. When Pond finished explaining his plans, Alexander volunteered to accompany him. The older man accepted the offer.

Alexander left Fort Detroit for Montreal, his mind seething. Believing his whole life had been lived in preparation for great events yet to come, he was determined to accompany Pond in the search for the northwest passage. Together they would acquire vast fortunes and imperishable glory. Together they would inaugurate a new era in human history.

But a tremendous obstacle stood between Alexander Mackenzie and his goal. The most powerful of all the senior partners in the North-West Company disliked him. Simon McTavish, the wealthiest of Montreal's pedlars, was a dour, single-minded fur trader who had spent a half-century in the industry. Now chairman of North-West's board of directors, he had reluctantly allowed his partners to persuade him that Alexander was worth promoting.

The young man knew how his superior felt. Alexander wanted change, but McTavish stood for the *status quo*. Alexander was a radical who dreamed of new worlds to conquer. "The Marquis," as McTavish was called, thought it a foolish waste of time and money to seek an overland route to the Pacific. And Alexander even carried in his wallet an order, signed by McTavish, directing his subordinates to concentrate solely on the development of the vast Athabaska basin — later to become the huge provinces of Alberta and Saskatchewan.

Soon after Alexander reached Montreal, he attended a staff meeting at which McTavish presided. The old man, irritable and dictatorial as always, set forth a new policy. In twenty or thirty years, he said, when every man now active in North-West had retired, a new, younger breed could search for the pot of gold at the end of the rainbow. McTavish himself preferred the tangible gold of the here and now.

Alexander wisely kept his own plans to himself, confiding in no one except Roderic. Not daring to cross his powerful superior, he decided to proceed cautiously. His first step was to get into physical condition for the trials that awaited him. His trip to Fort Detroit having been successful, he applied for permission to make a longer journey to Grand Portage at the western end of Lake Superior, the real gateway to the northwest. The company had built a major trading post there, a senior partner was in command, and a full company of guards, all of them former soldiers, kept the peace. There, too, the warehouses were piled with furs from dirt floors to timbered ceilings, scores of *voyageurs* rested and quarreled, brawled and sometimes killed each other, and Indians of many tribes came there to exchange skins for blankets, iron pots — and rum.

Alexander's application was approved and he set out early in the summer of 1786. From the start, his journey was unorthodox. He refused to make himself comfortable amidships in a bateau. Instead, he placed himself in the lead canoe. Wielding a paddle, he set a grueling pace, starting out on each day's voyage at three o'clock in the morning and refusing to make camp until long after sundown. The *voyageurs* were used to halting every two hours to smoke a pipe. Alexander made no change in their routine, but at every stop he himself scribbled in a notebook, recording his impressions of all that he had seen.

The men thought him mad. Never before had they encountered a *bourgeois* who slaved over a paddle like a *voyageur*. They did not realize, of course, that he was in training for adventures yet to come.

From the onset he demonstrated a natural instinct for leadership. A strict disciplinarian, he was never unfair and always did more than his share of the work. He rationed the men liberal quantities of rum every night, although he himself drank no hard spirits. And he broke precedent by giving the men smoking tobacco paid for out of his own pocket.

Yet he refused to fraternize with them. He slept apart and ate all of his meals at a small, private campfire built for his sole use. He rarely rested for any length of time, and in his spare moments kept writing copious notes in his pad. Scores of expeditions had already journeyed to Grand Portage, but Alexander was the first to write in detail about the topography, the wild life, and the scenery. The Indians fascinated him, so did the trees; in fact, he treasured everything he saw, heard and smelled. The years spent sitting at a desk rolled away; he knew he had come into his own element.

Surprised to discover that the Michilimackinac Indians used tiny arrows, he ferreted out their secret. The tips were steeped in a poison made by boiling the root of a plant found on Mackinac Island. The slightest scratch caused death; these natives did not need large arrows to kill their foes.

The whitefish of Lake Superior, he declared enthusiastically, were the best in the world. Delicious and nourishing when broiled, they retained their natural oils when smoked, keeping for indefinite periods. Alexander even tried to make whitefish pemmican; he was keenly disappointed when the attempt failed.

Alexander saw that birch trees grew in abundance everywhere, so bark was always available to make replacements for the canoes destroyed by careless *voyageurs*. When a new canoe was needed, Alexander himself undertook the task of making it, learning by trial and error how to shape the frame, cover it with bark, and use the gum of maples and evergreens to hold the craft together. And in his spare time, he had the *voyageurs* teach him all the Indian dialects they knew.

He was awed by the vast number of animals he saw. Enormous herds of buffalo grazed everywhere on the plains; Alexander believed a supply of meat was assured to all who traveled in the West for centuries to come. He shot deer and elk and bear, but found that bear meat grows rancid so quickly that, to prevent spoilage, it should be cooked or smoked immediately after the beast is slaughtered. The Huron Indians considered bear steak a delicacy. Alexander didn't agree with them; he believed that bear bacon was best suited to the palate of civilized men.

Blackberries grew in abundance on the northern shore of Lake Superior, but Alexander learned that they caused stomach disturbances when eaten before ripening. His conviction that the *voyageurs* behaved like children was strengthened when the men persisted in eating the green berries. He prevented them forcibly from gorging themselves.

By the time the expedition reached Grand Portage, Alexander was a veteran leader who knew his business.

At the post, trading occupied much of his time, but his real mission remained uppermost in his mind. He spent many hours interviewing Indians and *voyageurs* who had traveled north of Lake Winnipeg, bombarding them with countless, searching questions. And although he was tempted to travel up into Peter Pond's Athabaska domain, the shadow of Simon McTavish was long. A premature act might ruin the future. So Alexander resisted the urge. He was content to send Pond a long letter to be delivered by a junior clerk planning an expedition north, while he and his party headed back to Montreal.

Early frosts made travel less comfortable as Alexander and his party set out. The *voyageurs* grumbled when snow fell for three days and nights. But the young leader was delighted; the experience of traveling across snow and ice was precious. He was so eager to learn that he scarcely slept at all. When he arrived in Montreal, his boats were laden with furs and his notebooks for his great adventure were bulging. He was ready now, physically, intellectually, and emotionally.

The chance came in 1787. A letter of far-reaching consequence arrived at North-West's headquarters from Peter Pond, now in his forty-eighth year. Pond was in ill health and intended to retire as soon as he trained his replacement. In his letter he said that he knew the partners would select a man of their own choice. However, he urged Simon McTavish to consider the qualifications of the company's youngest *bourgeois*, Alexander Mackenzie.

McTavish and the other partners had no chance to ponder the matter because Alexander immediately volunteered for the post. Indeed, he showed such enthusiasm that no one else was even considered. And since it would not have been easy to persuade a wealthy, mature man, used to the comforts of Montreal, to accept a bleak, lonely exile in the wilderness, the partners were delighted that Alexander wanted the place. They elected him unanimously to replace Pond.

Alexander realized full well that Pond could not accompany him on the search for the northwest passage. He was not afraid, however, to make the attempt alone. Still keeping his plans secret, he arranged with Roderic to join him the following spring. He intended to leave his cousin in charge of trading operations while he himself set out on a journey into the unknown.

Setting his affairs in order as rapidly as possible, Alexander traveled into the Athabaska country, going to the northeastern comer of Alberta near the Saskatchewan border, more than eighteen hundred miles northwest of Grand Portage. Then, still fresh after his long journey, he persuaded Pond to show him the surrounding area. They made a number of journeys together through the countryside before snow and ice compelled them to return to Pond's cabin.

Spending the long winter there, Alexander absorbed all the new information his friend had gleaned. Indians spoke of a river running out of Great Slave Lake to the west; they swore it crossed a barrier of mountains, then flowed into the Pacific. Alexander intended to find that river and follow it to its outlet.

Housebound at the hut on the Athabaska River, Pond and Alexander spent most of their time before a roaring fire. The older man talked incessantly and Alexander listened. The veteran spoke of his lifetime's experiences; Alexander made notes, reducing to paper every scrap of information that might prove useful.

Pond knew a dozen ways of patching a leaking canoe, and how to find hidden, edible roots. He was familiar with the habits, customs and characteristics of a score of Indian nations. Alexander wrote until his fingers ached. Pond discussed the terrain he had explored; Alexander produced maps. Together they traced every river, every band of hills, every lake and portage.

When the snow began to melt, Pond packed his personal belongings, gave his successor a great bear hug and departed for the east. He would travel to Montreal where he would squander his fortune, and from there would return to his native Connecticut where he was destined to die in obscure poverty.

Alexander was on his own now, the supreme authority of North-West in a limitless wilderness. Unafraid and eager, he braced himself to meet the future he had sought.

IV: PRELUDE TO ADVENTURE

BY THE LATE SPRING of 1789, Alexander Mackenzie was ready to launch a great adventure. If his theories and those of Peter Pond were right, he would find the passage to the Pacific Ocean.

He had established a large, comfortable headquarters on the southern shore of Lake Athabaska in Alberta, calling it Fort Chipewyan — a name it has kept to the present day — after the Indian nation inhabiting the area. He had already initiated a vigorous trade with the natives, and Roderic, after making the journey of more than eighteen hundred miles north from Grand Portage, was now in charge of commercial operations. Roderic was really more than an assistant. He was a fellow-conspirator, because Mackenzie had had to hide his plans from Simon McTavish, who sat in his far-distant Montreal office counting his profits.

At Alexander's direction, smaller posts were established on the Peace River to the west in Alberta and at Slave Lake to the north, in the present-day territory of Mackenzie. At both sites, as at Lake Athabaska, the fishing was excellent. This was of prime importance, for game vanished in the winter months, and the senior clerks in charge of the posts depended on fish for fresh food.

The traders followed Mackenzie's careful instructions, and in their dealings with the Chipewyan, Slaves, Red-knives, and other tribes, asked countless questions about the unknown territory. The replies, mostly meager scraps of information, were written down and submitted to Alexander, who studied every word. When not otherwise occupied, he made a careful investigation of the sources of food, for he could not carry enough with him on his journey of exploration to feed his entire party for week after week. He had to depend on the land and water.

According to all that he gleaned, the signs were favorable. The lakes were well stocked with whitefish; they spawned in the autumn, then crowded in shoals to the shallow water when the frosts came. So there would be plenty of whitefish. Equally important was the fact that hardy *voyaguers* who traveled in the northwest were accustomed to a diet of white-fish. If necessary, they could eat the same dish without salt or other seasoning at every meal.

In the spring and again in the autumn, for short periods of time great numbers of wild fowl flew overhead. The hunter with a good eye and steady hand could then bring down almost unlimited quantities of ducks, geese, pheasant, quail, partridge, and other birds.

In the summer — but only then, venison and elk, buffalo and an occasional bear could be shot. However, these animals were found for such a brief time that Alexander feared he could not depend on their meat. He did not expect to find much game in the raw wilderness of the far north and west. According to the Indians, the area was uninhabited by men or beasts, therefore, large supplies of pemmican were brought north from Grand Portage for the journey.

Alexander had, in his possession, Pond's crude maps and several of his own, but he alone knew that no two sketches were alike. The *voyageurs* might mutiny if they realized their leader had no idea of what lay beyond the next hill or the next bend in a river. A few days before departing, Mackenzie confided in Henry Fuller Bishop, a young boy from New Haven. This lad, seeking a life of excitement, had come north on his own initiative. Bishop was all the more anxious to make the journey after being told the truth.

Alexander had personally designed the four canoes that would carry the members of the expedition. The largest of them was his own, thirty-two feet long. It was four feet, ten inches wide, in the middle and narrowed to two feet, six inches fore and aft. Made of yellow birchbark he had selected himself, it was stretched taut, without a single wrinkle, over seventy-one ribs of thin but resilient white cedar. The longitudinal slats were of cedar, too, and the canoe was so spacious that it could carry twenty-five pieces of trading goods and pemmican, in addition to the crew, their provisions, and gear.

The cargo included blankets, knives, and other merchandise suitable as presents for any strange Indian tribes the expedition might encounter. Each man carried his own rifle, pistols and knives, ammunition and powder. But spare rifles were provided for all, as well as considerable quantities of extra ammunition and shot. Each of the canoes carried a mast of oak and a stout sail of double-sewn canvas. And there were iron-tipped setting-poles for every man. Also tents and blankets and kettles, towing-lines and *watape*, a natural vine used to sew rips in the bark of the canoes. There were skin containers of gum to seal leaks in the vessels, hatchets, and the ever-useful crooked knives that Indians liked so well. Ninety-pound pieces of pemmican and others of jerked venison and parched corn provided an adequate food supply. The cargoes were covered with cloths soaked in corn oil and animal fat to make them waterproof.

Mackenzie's canoe contained four *voyageurs* and three other passengers in addition to Alexander himself. Two were Indian wives of *voyageurs*. The third was a young German scientist and adventurer, John Steinbruck of Cologne, who had come to the

New World seeking a different sort of life than he had known as a university graduate student.

A Chipewyan leader known as English Chief rode in the second canoe; Alexander had engaged him as guide, interpreter, and principal hunter. Two of his wives rode with him as did young Bishop. Indian paddlers provided the manpower. Other members of English Chief's tribe occupied the third canoe.

Laurent LeRoux, a senior clerk of the North-West Company and second-in-command of the expedition, brought up the rear in the fourth canoe, together with four more *voyageurs*.

On June 2, 1789, all was in readiness for departure. Then a sudden rainstorm caused a delay. English Chief and his warriors were superstitious; they refused to leave until the sun was shining. The departure was delayed until the following day.

The sun shone brightly on June 3, but last-minute difficulties prevented the party from setting out as early as planned. A large crowd was gathered at Fort Chipewyan; junior clerks, *voyageurs* resting there, and two traders from Grand Portage mingled with the braves and squaws of the Chipewyan tribe.

As LeRoux shouted an order, the *voyageurs* and warriors making the journey took their places in the canoes. Alexander had shown his usual foresight; each man had been given only one small beaker of rum.

Had they been allowed to consume as much as they wanted, there would have been still another delay, and Alexander could not afford to lose time. By the end of September at the latest, the stinging cold of winter would envelop the country, making further travel impossible. Alexander could only count on four months for his journey. If he failed to reach the Pacific in two and one-half months, he would be compelled to turn back, then resume his explorations the following year. So every day was precious.

The employees of North-West and the Chipewyan shouted as Alexander emerged from the Fort accompanied by young Bishop. Walking quickly to the canoes, they paused briefly to shake the hands thrust at them. A volley of musket fire echoed through the wilderness. Then, when Alexander raised and lowered his pole, the oarsmen went to work with a vengeance.

By noon the Fort had disappeared off to the east; the course was changed from due west to northwest. The explorers were traveling now through familiar waters, those of Lake Athabaska, also a present-day name, which empties into the River des Rochers. On this first day the men had made a run of thirty-seven miles, only a taste of what was to come. Thereafter they would start at four o'clock every morning and paddle until seven at night. They would travel at least four miles an hour and often as fast as ten.

Work did not end, of course, when the day's journey was completed. Fires were started and the canoes, after being hauled ashore, were inspected in their light. Any cracks in them must be gummed. Then, too, tents had to be erected and preparations made for an early start the next day.

The party dined sumptuously that first night on grilled whitefish, roasted goose and the boiled root of a plant called *oraki* by the Chipewyan. Young Bishop thought the vegetable tasted like turnips, but Steinbruck found it bitter and unpalatable.

At four o'clock the next morning the canoes started out again. Soon they were on the Slave River. Here the river is about one thousand yards wide and the current is steady at three miles per hour. The *voyageurs* and warriors did little real work, for the current carried them.

The following morning paddling became more demanding. At the point the party had reached, the river falls nearly one hundred and fifty feet in sixteen miles. Intricate channels, with ugly rocks beneath the boiling surface and logjams of driftwood, add to the difficulty of water travel. Six large rapids and a number of smaller ones had to be passed, so the strength of every member of the party was strained to the breaking point.

Seven portages had to be made now, the shortest of them about three hundred yards, the longest more than twelve hundred. On all but one, the men had to unload the cargo and carry their equipment and ninety-pound pieces as well as the canoes. The craft were hoisted onto the shoulders of the bowsmen and steersmen. The two men from Alexander's canoe had a particularly arduous task for it weighed more than three hundred pounds. Only one of the rapids was small enough for the canoes to be hauled through the water attached to lead ropes, and parts of the cargoes had to be removed to lighten them.

The rapids were not the only troubles plaguing the expedition. Mosquitoes, traveling in such dense clouds that they sometimes obliterated the sun, tormented the travelers both on shore and on the water. Everyone was bitten repeatedly. The *voyageurs* wanted to anoint themselves with rum to ease the itching and burning of their skin, but Alexander restrained them. He knew that the sugar in the liquor would attract still more mosquitoes.

In the days that followed, the men's discomfort became more acute. A cold wind blew in from the northwest, driving the temperature down close to freezing. There were squalls several days in a row, then rain fell steadily. Nights were spent now on soggy ground under dripping tents. The weather became too wet to light fires, the explorers huddled under blankets, trying in vain to keep warm and dry.

Alexander was apparently impervious to the elements; every evening he crouched over his notebooks in the dark and jotted down his day's observations.

After following a small river that twisted, turned, and meandered in endless loops, the boats were paddled into Great Slave Lake, the huge body of water that extends, roughly, from the 61st to the 63rd degree of latitude in the southern portion of the mammoth Northwest Territory of Mackenzie.

To the infinite relief of the men, the mosquitoes, after bothering them for days, suddenly disappeared. The explorers soon learned the reason for this. It was so early in the season that the lake was completely frozen except along the banks. Alexander, going ashore, found that the ground had thawed to the depth of only fourteen inches.

The hunting, however, was excellent. The men shot beaver, swans and geese, and later found moose, caribou, and buffalo, smaller than the great plains animals seen farther south. No one went hungry now. Large supplies were even left on the shore of the lake at a hut built the previous year by LeRoux. It had occurred to Alexander that they might need food after returning from unknown parts.

Suddenly the mosquitoes came back in great swarms. Only Alexander considered their presence a favorable sign. His estimate proved correct, for a strong wind blew the fast-breaking ice up onto the shore. The fishing nets had been covered; they had to be dug out now. But no one minded the work, for it was plain that the spring thaws were at hand.

With the warmer weather came a northern electrical storm. One day, in mid-morning, the sky overhead turned so dark that the men had to beach the boats. Then a brilliant bolt of lightning made the entire area as bright as noon under a brilliant sun. The bolt vanished, and a few seconds later the earth trembled as the roar of a thunderbolt echoed through the wilderness.

Heavy rain began to fall. Somewhere in the distance a huge tree crashed to earth. Alexander, aware of lightning's affinity for water, ordered the boats hauled high onto the shore. It was raining so hard that the men could not see more than a few feet before their faces and the ice underfoot was melting so rapidly they kept losing their balance.

Another flash lighted the area, then a second crash of thunder sounded. It was so much closer that English Chief and the other Indians ducked their heads beneath their arms in terror. Then the lightning and thunder became almost continuous. The men were blinded and deafened; Alexander himself felt dazed. A thirty-foot poplar, standing a short distance away, was struck by lightning; it burned fiercely even though the rain was coming down harder than ever. The Indians were terrified, but their wails were lost in the rumble of thunder. Rocks crashed into the lake as the rain melted the ice. Alexander felt as if the nether regions of Hell had risen to the surface of the earth.

The storm continued unabated for more than four hours. When the sky finally cleared, the members of the party were too exhausted to resume their journey. The canoes needed gumming, everyone was soaked to the skin, and mosquitoes added to the explorers' misery.

But there were compensations — at least for Alexander. That night the atmosphere was so clear he could read without a candle or an oil lamp. He was so elated he spent the entire night checking his notebooks.

When the journey was begun again, Alexander took lessons from English Chief in the Indian dialects of the north. His ear for languages being acute, he was soon able to converse with the other Indians in the party. But the dialects of wandering bands later encountered on the journey proved beyond his grasp.

Nevertheless, he was determined to reach the northern shores of Great Slave Lake. His desire to push on was spurred by the mosquitoes. They continued to make life miserable for the entire party even though the boats were surrounded almost constantly by floating cakes of ice.

Then, on a small island, young Bishop discovered large quantities of cranberries and small, strong-tasting scallions. Alexander promptly gave the party something to think about other than mosquitoes. From his own boyhood privations, he knew that a balanced diet promoted good health far better than a monotonous one. So now he insisted that the *voyageurs* eat both the raw scallions and the cranberries boiled by the squaws. The men were indignant but obeyed, and then spent several hours complaining of indigestion. Ignoring their grumbling, Alexander was heartened when a strong south wind sprang up. The ice pack was driven toward the north, leaving a considerable area clear. Alexander estimated that they were only three miles from the northern shore of the lake. Unfortunately, the intervening area was filled with broken, dangerous ice.

Another delay was inevitable, so the men went off on their own to hunt, returning with two small caribou. Alexander, busy with charts and maps, named the island Ile de Carreboeuf. He devoted that entire night to making astronomical calculations, and not until much later did he realize he knew so little about the science of astronomy that his observations were almost meaningless.

At dawn it was seen that a crust of ice one-half inch thick had formed on the surface of the water. The sun melted it, however, and the voyage was resumed, the party traveling thirteen miles toward the northwest along the fringe of the ice pack. That night on the island where they halted, LeRoux buried two bags of pemmican. Two trees were cut down, stripped, and lashed together to make a flagpole identifying the spot. Alexander believed that the pemmican would prove useful on the return voyage.

He named the island Ile a la Cache and marked his maps and charts accordingly. The weather was bitter cold, but the mosquitoes had reappeared in great swarms, and everyone was glad to shove off again when the crust of ice melted. Two days later, the explorers crossed to the mainland.

There they found a lodge of the Red-Knives, who told them there were two other native houses in the immediate vicinity. Alexander and LeRoux acquired a large number of beaver and marten skins in return for iron cooking pots and knives, several lengths of rope and some blankets. Alexander was anxious to learn something about the river he was seeking, a river that would carry them to the Pacific. So he gave the Red-Knives a jug of rum.

The chiefs said they knew nothing about the river, but two of the warriors, the tribe's principal hunters, claimed they could find the stream. Immediately engaging the warriors as guides, Alexander bought a canoe from the Red-Knives to transport them. Then, suspecting that the copper used by the natives for making their weapons was valuable, he obtained several of their knives and wrote a long description of their nearby mines.

The party of explorers now broke into two groups. LeRoux remained behind alone, to pursue his trade with the Indians. After he had obtained enough furs, he was to make his way back to Fort Chipewyan. Meanwhile, Alexander and his companions pushed on, led by their new guides. They crossed a deep bay, the north arm of Great Slave Lake, dotted with many islands, and, traveling north and east, came again to the mainland. The countryside differed greatly now from that to which they had grown accustomed. Instead of rocks and moss-covered valleys, the party saw loose, sandy soil. Farther to the north on a gradually rising plateau, were deep woods reminding the men of vast forests two thousand miles to the south.

The guides now led them on a dizzy, ever-changing course. They paddled forty-five miles toward the southeast, traveling along the west side of the lake's north arm. Occasionally they appeared to be lost, and twice the Red-Knives led them into deep bays, then doubled back. English Chief was convinced that the guides, whose tribe had been feuding for generations with his Chipewyan, intended to kill him. Wanting to strike first, he threatened to murder both the Red-Knives.

Alexander felt compelled to halt the fight before it became serious enough to jeopardize the safety of the entire party. He insisted that all the natives give him their firearms. English Chief and the Chipewyan refused, so he drew his pistols and faced them in the open. Bishop and Steinbruck flanked him, their own rifles ready. English Chief then realized that the leader meant what he said.

The weapons were surrendered and their owners did not get them back until the following night, after a ceremony in which all the Indians swore in the name of their ancestors not to shed blood. Alexander calmly accepted their word, but made it plain that he himself would execute anyone who did not live up to his pledge.

The rest of the voyage on Great Slave Lake was uncertain and tense. The guides confessed that they had not visited the region in eight years. But at last they saw a deep stand of rushes at the entrance to a bay. Both the warriors were certain then that they were heading in the right direction.

At four o'clock in the morning on Monday, June 29, the party started out on the last leg of its journey to the mythical river. After spending twenty days on Great Slave Lake, they left it, entering a narrow channel no more than six feet deep on the north side of a large island. The channel was filled with so many fish that, without even leaving their canoes, the *voyageurs* speared quite a number. There were also birds of all kinds. The Indians considered their presence a good omen.

The channel moved in a straight line toward the north; it obviously must be an outlet from the lake. At midday the explorers moved out of the channel and came at last to the river, marked on Peter Pond's map but charted nowhere else. Alexander, calling a halt, tried to fix the precise spot on the new map he himself was making.

Pond had been right and the Red-Knives had not been dreaming. The river was indeed real. Steinbruck, Bishop, and the *voyageurs* realized they were taking part in a history-making event. They watched in awed silence as Alexander wrote in his notebook that he had found the headwaters of the Grand River.

They did not, however, like the name he chose. Among themselves, they preferred to call it the Mackenzie River.

V: THE RIVER AND THE MOUNTAINS

PETER POND had proved so accurate regarding the existence of a great river in the northwest, one originating north of Great Slave Lake, that Alexander Mackenzie's first reaction was to banish from his mind any remaining doubts about the rest of his ideas. The river, Pond had told him, flowed toward the southwest. On it were located the largest falls in the known world. Cutting through a northern spur of the rugged north-south range known as the Rocky Mountains, the stream made its way between gorges and ravines, narrow valleys and hidden lowlands, and emerged on the western side. From that point it flowed in a straight line toward the Pacific.

In spite of his high hopes, however, Alexander remained a realist. He questioned the Red-Knives closely about falls on the river. At first the Indians hesitated, but they finally agreed that they existed. He was elated until English Chief came to him privately and said that the guides were being amenable only because they wanted a reward. They knew no more than anyone else about such falls in his opinion.

So Alexander discarded Pond's theories. His friend had been right about the existence of the river, but now it would be a mistake to rely on mere conjecture. A meeting was called on the bank of the river, and Alexander explained to his followers, first in English, then in French, and finally in the Chipewyan dialect, that no one really knew where the river led. Anyone who was fearful and wanted to turn back could leave at once.

Bishop and Steinbruck had no intention of returning east, and the *voyageurs* insisted to a man on accompanying their leader. The Chipewyan would not think of abandoning the venture, and the Red-Knives proudly insisted that they had earned the right to lead the expedition.

Tears came to Alexander's eyes as he thanked his companions for their faith in him. He promised to do his best for all of them, no matter what lay ahead.

Excitement ran high now as the canoes, spurred by a moderate current, sailed past an island about fourteen miles long. For a time they traveled due west, then southwest. Alexander wondered what kind of magic Pond had employed. No civilized man, indeed no Indian known to civilized men had ever traveled in these waters, yet Pond's theory seemed accurate. Alexander wondered again about the great falls; his uncertainty tormented him.

On both sides of the river the countryside was very low, the river itself so broad that a man could hardly see from one bank to the other. Alexander realized that his party had come into another lake. He made several unsuccessful attempts to find his way out, at last locating the main channel which flowed toward the south.

The area to the north was heavily forested; it seemed to be a low plain. To the south, the leader saw a plateau more sparsely wooded. He could not help wondering whether he was heading toward the spur of the Rockies, the last great barrier standing between him and the Pacific.

When the journey was resumed, the river flowed almost due south. Excitement mounted again when a ridge of low mountains was sighted directly ahead. A new river teeming with trout emptied into the Mackenzie. Alexander marked it on his map as the Trout River, a name by which it has since been known. The party camped there for the night.

The sluggish waters ended a few miles below the Trout River camp, the river narrowing to a width of half a mile. The current increased to about eight miles per hour. Alexander, haunted by fears of falls, frequently paused to take soundings. In the afternoon he lost his lead and part of his sounding line. It was severed by an underwater portion of an ice floe. Ice indeed was piled high on both banks of the river.

To the extreme disappointment of the entire party, the river now turned north and west again, then due north. Hopes of finding an immediate passage to the Pacific faded. Near the junction of another river was a small island with signs of previous habitation — the framework of four separate native lodges.

After the Chipewyan and Red-Knives had examined the site for some time, they decided that the island had been inhabited by people of the Knisteneau nation better known as the Cree. This was a fierce tribe of warriors much feared by all other Indians. There was no way of determining how long a time had elapsed since the Cree had left the island, but Alexander guessed that the lodges had been abandoned at least ten years earlier.

The Chipewyan wanted to go home now, but hated to appear cowardly before the Red-Knives; the two guides themselves, although visibly upset, made no mention of leaving. Alexander was less worried about the Cree than he was about the possibility of coming to the falls unexpectedly. So he ordered another quantity of pemmican buried on the island, explaining that it would be used on the return voyage. The Indians were unable to share his optimism; they felt positive that the winter would be spent in the unknown wilderness. They declared openly that they did not expect to return in less than a year.

The tools and weapons the Cree had left behind them created mixed emotions in Alexander. The natives obviously had not been acquainted with iron, so if he found some Cree villages, he could do a great deal of business with them. The trader in him rejoiced; he hoped to get large quantities of furs in return for firearms and iron knives. On the other hand, his sense of disappointment was far greater, for he reasoned that if the Cree had no iron tools, they had not come in contact with explorers on the Pacific coast.

Late one morning a vast range of snow-capped mountains appeared to the west and south when the sun burned away the haze. The range stretched as far as the explorers could see. Studying the slopes with care, they made out wooded patches, but saw, too, that a great many of the peaks soared high above the timber line. Most of the summits were lost in clouds.

Alexander immediately called a halt, studied the mountains through his telescope, and scribbled furiously in his notebook. Even the Indians sensed his excitement. The *voyageurs* wanted to celebrate with rum, a suggestion that was refused.

No explorer could have known a more thrilling moment. Alexander had discovered a vast range of towering mountains totally unknown to civilized man. Even in those first exhilarating moments, he realized that he had won immortality.

Few men in any age have duplicated his twin feat of finding both a great river and a sprawling chain of mountains. The Mackenzie River, the second longest on the North American continent, extends approximately fifteen hundred miles from Great Slave Lake to the Arctic Ocean into which it empties. Its total length, including that of the Peace River, its greatest branch to the southwest, is considerably more than two thousand, five hundred miles. Its average width is greater than one mile, and when not in a flood stage, it discharges more than one-half million cubic feet of water per second. And, as Alexander himself learned, it is navigable for about four months a year, freezing in October and thawing in late May and early June.

The Mackenzie Mountains stagger the imagination, too. The range lies directly to the west of the river, running parallel to it for approximately one thousand miles. Alexander believed them to be separate and distinct from the Rocky Mountains, and he was right. His instincts proved superior to the logic of scholars who, in the years immediately after his stunning discovery, assumed the chain to be the northernmost spur of the Rockies.

As Alexander peered through his telescope, he knew that he had entered an unchartered world. He was responsible for reporting his findings to scientists with accuracy and skill. He faced as well the almost superhuman task of drawing intelligible maps for those who came after him. Never again would man entertain false ideas about the northwestern portion of the continent.

For a time Alexander's mind churned. His notes were scribbled so hastily that he later had to rewrite them in a legible hand. Realizing at once that he had discovered a fabulous area for fur-trading, he assumed that the North-West Company would become far richer and more powerful. And even though he had no idea of the natural resources of the region, he wrote in his notebook that many minerals of value must lie here below the surface of the earth.

Steinbruck later said that the drama of the moment was intensified by the quiet. For the better part of an hour, there was no sound but the rushing of water and the scratching of Alexander's quill pen. Even the voluble *voyageurs* were reduced to an awed silence. Bishop later told his parents that he felt as Columbus must have felt when his squadron of tiny ships reached the Caribbean.

Alexander himself was the first to recover his poise. He was certain, he said, that the others shared his curiosity. Now it was their duty to find where the river would lead and to discover, if possible, the size and extent of the mountain chain. That task would take many grueling days. And with the resources available, the little party could do no more than obtain a few basic facts as they traveled downstream into the unknown.

Portions of the rocky heights above the timber line were a brilliant, glistening white. Steinbruck, an amateur geologist, believed they were talc; young Bishop agreed with him. The Indians, however, thought the white parts were spirit stones and called them *manetoe aseniah*. Under no circumstances, they said, did they want to climb those peaks. Alexander calmly noted in his journal that he had seen snow on the heights.

The range had no name, so Steinbruck proposed that the peaks be called the Mackenzie Mountains. Alexander agreed to mark them on his map accordingly, but said he preferred a more suitable, permanent name.

The current averaged now about four miles per hour, and the banks rose sharply to a height of about two hundred feet on each side. Alexander thought constantly of Pond's great rapids, so the party proceeded with great caution, pausing every time anyone heard a sound hinting that they were approaching falls.

But they encountered no difficulty. The river turned sharply toward the north after meandering for several miles. Then it widened, the current increased to about seven or eight miles per hour, and the banks dropped away. There were many islands in this part of the river, one of them at least twenty miles long.

Some hours after the mountains had been sighted, the Indians came to Alexander in a group to complain that the pace was too swift. He commented mildly that they had been traveling only seventy-five miles per day and reminded them that the *voyageurs*, who were anything but unhappy, were capable of attaining a far greater speed.

For the moment the Indians said no more, but retired in sullen silence. Alexander knew, of course, that he had been less than fair in using the *voyageurs* as an example to shame and discipline them. Years of experience enabled the French-Canadians to work as long as twenty hours in twenty-four. The *voyageurs* were content to eat unsalted meat and fish, to drink a dram of whisky or rum in the morning and another at night, to endure physical hardships of every description, because they had a personal stake in the venture. If a northwest passage was discovered, their financial reward would be considerable; besides they would share in Mackenzie's glory. Furthermore, they would take their ease through the long winter months.

But the Chipewyan and Red-Knives had no use either for money or for glory. If Alexander was pleased with their work, he would give them gifts of weapons and blankets, but they would not acquire greater prestige in their own tribes, and they were indifferent to the acclaim of the outside world. They completely lacked the spirit of adventure that motivated men from the civilized world; they cared only about their immediate creature comforts.

Still Alexander knew he needed their help. Understanding their discontent, he took immediate steps to placate them. And now when their complaints ceased, he opened a package containing weapons and presented each Indian with a new pistol. At the same time he made them understand that in the future he would not be subjected to blackmail. Any native who was dissatisfied could leave whenever he wished.

This strong stand impressed the Indians far more than the pistols. Retiring to a spot some distance from the river, they conferred earnestly for an hour or more. Then English Chief came to Alexander and, admitting that he and the others had lost face, offered to return the weapons. Alexander blandly refused. The incident was closed.

It was fortunate indeed that peace had been restored, for the party needed all its courage and stamina. The bluffs on both sides of the river grew higher; and before the explorers entirely realized what was happening, they saw that the river was cutting through the high mountains. The stream narrowed from a width of one and one-half miles to one-half mile or less, the current increased to a rate of about ten miles per hour and many rocks jutted out of the water. The oarsmen needed all their skill to avoid striking a rock and smashing a canoe.

Fear of rapids ahead became greater. The water boiled constantly, then everyone heard a noise sounding like the hissing of a kettle. No one could explain it; the Indians became frightened. The gods of the river, they said, were angry and threatening to destroy them.

Alexander studied the water with great care. He concluded finally that the sound, which the members of the expedition actually felt rather than heard, was caused by particles of loose sand being forced up against the hulls of the boats. Steinbruck, who had also been studying the phenomenon, agreed with the leader's analysis.

Several days later, a party of Slave and Dog-Rib Indians appeared. Alexander questioned the band at length about the country into which he was heading. The replies were not encouraging. It would take several winters to reach the sea, the Indians said, and old age would come upon every member of the party before the return voyage could be made. Adding that fierce monsters of horrible shapes would be encountered on the river, they talked at length about the destructive power of these beasts. When asked about rapids, they said there were two enormous falls on the river, both of them impassable. The closer was less than thirty days' march away.

Plainly the natives were uttering sheer nonsense. Alexander discounted virtually everything he had been told. But his own Indians became alarmed and, already tired of the journey, begged him to turn back at once. When he refused, they told him the Slaves and Dog-Ribs had informed them privately that game and fish were so scarce in the country ahead that the entire party would die of starvation if no other calamity struck first.

Alexander still insisted he would continue; he persuaded one of the Dog-Rib braves to accompany the expedition. As payment in advance for his services, the man accepted a small kettle, an axe, a large hunting knife, and several other articles.

In the next few days, progress downstream was rapid. Hordes of mosquitoes reappeared to annoy the party, but hunting was good and everyone ate heartily. The ever-present, rugged mountains continued to line both banks of the river; some of the men felt hemmed in.

When the rapids were finally discovered, Alexander went ashore with English Chief to study them before advancing further. The drop was fairly steep on the east side of the river where numerous rocks made boat travel dangerous, but on the western side the descent was so gradual that the party was able to continue by canoe. The Dog-Rib guide insisted stubbornly that the rapids were dangerous. Alexander became annoyed. Tales of falls, he more than suspected, were greatly exaggerated.

In any event, he marked the spot on his map — a short distance north of a river flowing from the west into the main stream. He named this the Carcajou River, for near the junction was a one-thousand foot rock vaguely resembling a wolverine.

Alexander was privately worried because they were still traveling north. The mountains continued to stretch out toward the northern horizon. The fact that a river came in from the west was a sign that a considerable body of land lay in that direction. It might be necessary to go much farther before reaching the Pacific. Alexander began to have serious doubts about arriving there. His common sense told him that he was headed in the wrong direction.

Other natives were encountered from time to time, and one day the explorers met a large party very different from any of the other Indians they had seen. These warriors were strong, tall, and healthy. They kept their persons very clean. Strangely, English Chief understood everything they said, although the warriors could not make out one word of his language.

These people used a weapon unlike any that Alexander had seen. It was a bow made of two pieces with a very strong cord of sinew along the back. When this cord became wet, both a strong bowstring and a powerful arm were needed to draw it. Alexander thought that the bow might have been copied from the Eskimos.

He purchased a number of dressed moose skins from these Indians. They presented him with several delicious, unusual-looking fish. Smaller than a herring, the fish was spotted with black and yellow. Its dorsal fin reached from the head to the tail. Its mouth was armed with sharp, pointed teeth.

The Indian whose speech was most intelligible to Alexander and to English Chief was persuaded to accompany the party as a guide. The new guide said the sea was "ten sleeps" away; he promised that in "three sleeps" they would be in the land of the Eskimos. His people, he explained, had fought a long war against the Eskimos, but peace had been concluded the previous year. All the up-river Indians, he declared contemptuously, were old women and liars, and he had no use for the Slaves, Hares, or Dog-Ribs.

Soon after this, Steinbruck saw a beaver and shot it. The guide became frightened, his brothers too; none of them had ever heard the sound of firearms. Alexander persuaded them that it was a signal of friendship, and the guide then consented to embark, and several others accompanied the party in their own canoes for a short distance. They began to sing some of their songs, and, to the astonishment of the explorers, to fling themselves around in their boats.

The guide joined in this odd behavior, but his own small canoe was too cramped. He asked to be taken into Alexander's much larger boat. His request granted, he started immediately performing several violent Eskimo dances. Since Alexander and the *voyageurs* feared he would crash through the thin skin of the craft, they did their best to calm him. Finally he consented to sit down, but could not remain silent. He talked at great length about the Eskimos. They were a violent people, he said, and demonstrated his point by describing just how they had tortured his grandfather. The guide talked incessantly as the journey continued.

Alexander now found it impossible to believe that he was near the Pacific, for he had been traveling north rather than west most of the time. On the banks of the river he saw large fields of wild flax, the growth of the previous year, lying on the ground. New plants were sprouting up through the rotting vegetation. He marveled that flax should appear so unexpectedly.

The countryside behind low banks of clay had become flat, and no mountains were visible now. Alexander admitted to himself that he was confused.

On Friday, July 10, the canoes entered a section of the river that Alexander called the Narrows. On both sides of the Mackenzie the banks were high, and in the distance one could see snow-topped mountains whose peaks were barely visible. Again the fear of rapids haunted the party, but again none were found. Then suddenly the river widened. It spread in many channels among low islands, some of which were barren. Others were covered with spruce larger than any on the whole length of the Mackenzie. The low banks of the islands stood about six feet above the surface of the water; many were blanketed by sheets of clear ice beneath which could be seen rich, black earth.

The men now observed a strange phenomenon, both amusing and perplexing to them. As the ice melted beneath the summer sun, the ground around the trees near the water's edge suddenly gave way. The trees fell into the river, often carrying their roots with them. Alexander reasoned that, although they had died, they had been held upright for many months by the ice.

There were many channels in the river; the guide did not know which one to take. Alexander selected the middle channel. That night the party camped on the ice of an island. Alexander, taking his bearings, found he was much farther east than his compass had indicated. Although he could not understand why the instrument was behaving erratically, he felt certain that his observations were correct. He spent the rest of the night making calculations. As a result of his labors, he concluded that the river did not empty into the Pacific as he had hoped so fervently. Instead, he felt sure, it drained into the sea called by some the Hyperborean, known to others as the Arctic Ocean.

VI: DANGERS IN THE ARCTIC

ALEXANDER MACKENZIE did not dare tell his companions that they were near the Arctic Ocean. Steinbruck and Fuller had been deeply concerned for some time, and hearing the truth now would have thrown the *voyageurs* into a panic. As for the Indian guides and hunters, they already sensed that the party was far from its original goal.

The warrior who had recently joined the party kept terrifying the uneasy Chipewyan and Red-Knives with grave stories about impending dangers. The Eskimos, he said, were the crudest, most barbaric people on earth; they practiced cannibalism. He swore they had eaten alive a member of his own family.

But even if the explorers escaped murder or torture at the hands of the Eskimos, he said, their future remained bleak. The region ahead would yield no game, and even fish were scarce. Unless the party turned back soon, they all would perish.

A crisis exploded when the Indians came to Alexander, with English Chief acting as their spokesman, and begged him to abandon the journey.

He refused flatly.

They faced him defiantly, threatening to leave at once.

The situation was both delicate and tense. Alexander knew he could not afford to lose the services of the hunters and interpreters. But, at the same time, he would be unable to command their respect if he backed down now.

Bishop complicated the situation by drawing a loaded pistol, standing at the leader's side and telling the Indians to go about their business.

Alexander intervened, ordering Bishop to put away his pistol and take himself elsewhere for the moment. Firearms might cow the Chipewyan and Red-Knives, but they would bitterly resent a demonstration of force and would become even harder to handle. Therefore, it was better to deal with them as reasonably as possible.

Speaking slowly and quietly, Alexander called the Indians' bluff. If they wished to leave, he said, they were free to go. He would not try to detain them. In fact, he would give them a fair share of the food supplies. But he could not spare either ammunition or gunpowder, so their own rifles would be useless. Therefore, he added almost casually, if they left now, they probably would never see their homes again. They needed him to lead them.

The Indians had expected a long harangue; his simple speech took them by surprise. Alexander could see from their expressions that they knew he was right. Then he made them an unexpected, generous offer: if he did not reach the sea in seven days, he promised to turn back.

The Indians accepted his pledge, knowing that provisions were too low for him to break his word. The rebellion collapsed as quickly as it had flared. Everyone went back to work.

Alexander's own mind was seething. He was far from his original destination, yet could not halt short of the mouth of the river. There was territory still to be explored. Besides, he was bound and determined not only to see the unknown, but to make a complete map of the area and take back to the civilized world an accurate account of the region. In brief, he could not halt now.

The party continued down the channel, finding many old Eskimo camps. The men went ashore to examine some of them. Alexander surmised that, even though people had apparently lived in the dwellings for considerable periods of time, the Eskimos were nomads who moved on every year or two.

About the places where the Eskimos had made their fires the explorers found scattered pieces of whalebone, thick chunks of burned leather, and bits and pieces of several sturdy canoes. The huts were low and rounded, resembling strange domes. Made on frames of driftwood and covered with layers of tree branches and dried grass, they were topped with twelve to eighteen inches of earth.

Sledge runners and bars, pieces of whalebone and net floats made of bark were inside the houses and around the camps. Before each hut stood a large number of tree stumps fixed in the ground for use as fish racks.

On several islands Alexander and his men saw fresh footprints, but no Eskimos. Even so, the Indians became increasingly nervous. They were momentarily distracted by catching a glimpse of a black fox. Alexander encouraged a long discussion about the value of the animal's pelt. If the Indians could be led to think of furs, they might be less inclined to dwell on potential dangers.

The party made camp at an Eskimo bivouac that had been used that same year after the breaking of the ice pack. The miserable weather improved now and the sun came out brightly. The men went to bed in their tents after eating a dinner of fish and pemmican. Alexander remained out in the open; he was too excited to sleep.

Never before had he seen the sun so high in the sky at such a late hour. At midnight, still marveling, he roused the men in the closest tent. Bishop and one of the *voyageurs* soon joined him. Seeing the sun, they thought the company should embark and summoned the others. Alexander had great difficulty persuading his followers that the hour was really only a few minutes past midnight.

Alexander and Steinbruck then made careful calculations of the sun's position. The *voyageurs* were amused that there was no sunset, but the Indians, already fearful, now became completely terror-stricken.

When the voyage was resumed, the explorers seemed to have entered a weird new world. Willow trees stood but three feet high, spruces and pines were barely eighteen inches from top to bottom. There were no other trees of any kind.

The talkative guide chatted incessantly. At any minute now, he said, the party would come to a huge "lake." Eskimos lived on its shores. They subsisted on the meat of a creature part animal, part fish. Then, too, huge white bears, so strong that they could kill a dozen men with a single blow of a paw, roamed through the area. Often these fierce creatures seemed to appear suddenly, for the color of their fur blended perfectly with the white of the snow.

The guide also described another creature living in the waters of the "lake." Fortunately, no one could understand his words too clearly. Obviously, however, he was talking about some gargantuan beast far larger than any animal ever seen by the Chipewyans or Red-Knives.

The Indians were now on the thin edge of panic. Afraid they would bolt at any moment, Alexander called a halt. Staging an impressive ceremony, he gave English Chief one of his own coats. Made in Montreal, it was a handsome garment with pewter buttons and long lapels of deep maroon velvet. English Chief was delighted; he donned it at once.

The guide had to be satisfied, too, and, if possible, kept in a good humor. Because he had said many times that he considered the moose skins valuable, Alexander gave him one. The guide was elated, and when Alexander took him aside, he agreed to stop talking about the terrible dangers lying ahead.

The channels continued to wind and thread past naked, ice-covered islands, but a landing was made near a group of four dome-like huts which, the guide said, were Eskimo igloos.

The buildings stood on high ground. Alexander was amazed to see grass and tiny, delicate flowers of blue, yellow, and white growing there, for the ground was thawed no more than four inches from the surface. Beneath, there was solid ice.

Various objects found in the camp aroused Alexander's interest, too. There were small pieces of shaved flint attached to wooden handles with sinew; apparently the Eskimos used these weapons as knives. Alexander was impressed by cording made of willow bark; the men who had made the rope must have been extraordinarily patient. He was fascinated, too, by bits of tough, very thick leather. Neither his own Indians nor the guide could identify its origin. Alexander speculated that it might be the hide of sea horses but could not be certain, since he had never seen such creatures.

The explorers also came upon a stone kettle with a flat bottom. Alexander found that it held approximately two gallons of liquid. He wondered what tools the Eskimos had used to shape and hollow it out of solid, unyielding rock; the task must have been long and arduous. Alexander could not understand why after devoting so much labor to fashioning the kettle, the Eskimos had abandoned it.

The party finally entered the "lake," which Alexander guessed was in truth the Arctic Ocean. Uncertain where to go next, he directed the men to paddle toward the west. The canoes, moving out into the open, ice-filled water, headed toward the nearest spur of land fifteen miles distant. Upon reaching the promontory, the party found the body of water extending still farther to the west. But it was impossible to continue the voyage, for the water was never more than four feet deep and sometimes only one foot. Ice stretched out toward the horizon to the north, northeast, and northwest.

So reluctantly but sensibly, Alexander decided that he had reached the limit of his travels.

The party went ashore, the tents were erected, and English Chief supervised the setting of the fishing nets. Then Alexander, accompanied by the Chipewyan and Bishop, studied the area from the highest point of land in the vicinity. The water, he saw, was covered with solid ice for a distance of at least two leagues, or six miles. There was no sign of land anywhere. He knew then that his last hope of reaching the Pacific Ocean had vanished, but he did not feel depressed. For after all, he had not only traveled through thousands of miles of territory unknown to civilized man, but had made a series of important discoveries.

That knowledge, however, was insufficient to sustain him. Immediate, pressing problems demanded his attention. Food supplies were short, the weather was treacherous, and at any moment ferocious Eskimos might cause trouble. The long voyage upstream, taking the party back to civilization, loomed large in his mind. Skill and strength, courage and determination would be needed if they hoped to reach the safety of the far-distant home base.

On the night of Monday, July 13, forty days after leaving Fort Chipewyan, most of the men went to bed early. Alexander worked on his notebooks in his tent pitched on a hill some yards inland. But one of the *voyageurs*, sleeping in the tent closest to the shore, awoke when his blankets became soaked with salt water. Jumping to his feet, he lighted a candle in the darkened tent. Then, when he saw what was happening, he gave the alarm. The others roused themselves.

Alexander, having thrown down his notebooks, was the first to reach the shore. Water was creeping toward the precious sacks of food and bags of gunpowder. The boats, which had been secured by attaching lines to spikes driven in the ice, were now afloat and drifting. The tide had melted the ice.

He knew he had no one to blame but himself. The Arctic was an ocean so he should have remembered that tides were inevitable. If the food was destroyed now, the men would starve; if the gunpowder was soaked, they could neither defend themselves nor shoot game. And if they lost their boats, they would be trapped in the frozen wasteland of the north.

The boats were Alexander's first consideration. He waded to the nearest of them. Slipping and stumbling on the treacherous ice beneath the surface, he shouted an order to drag the supplies to higher ground. Then he climbed into the boat, snatched a paddle, and started toward another of the craft.

Within a few minutes he had rounded up all the canoes and, dragging them behind his own boat, paddled toward the shore. The waiting men beached the boats, hauling them far inland. The supplies were carried beyond the reach of the tide. The crisis ended less than a quarter of an hour after the first alarm had been given. A fire was lighted now to dry wet blankets as well as Alexander's boots. The men knew him well now, so no one was surprised to see him calmly resume work on his notebooks as he toasted his feet before the flames.

The weather turned remarkably mild the next day. A balmy breeze blew from the south and the sun was hot overhead. The explorers were in a cheerful mood. The nets yielded mixed blessings. They held seven inedible fish. The *voyageurs* called them *poissons inconnus*. There were also two large whitefish which the hungry men found delicious, and several other fish slightly smaller than herring. No one except English Chief could identify them. Saying that they were similar to a fish found in the waters of Hudson's Bay, he declared they made good eating. English Chief was proved right.

Alexander, making a careful count of the remaining provisions, found that they were reduced to about five hundred pounds. Since the party numbered fifteen persons, the food would last only twelve days if no other supplies were secured. It was necessary, obviously, to obtain other stores at once, so the nets were set again.

That morning, for the first time on the entire voyage, Alexander took his ease. His men were so surprised to find him lolling in his tent that they assumed he was ill, and he had to keep assuring them that he still enjoyed perfect health. His brief holiday came to an abrupt end late in the morning when two of the *voyageurs* reported excitedly that they had just seen several huge fish in the sea.

Alexander accompanied them to the shore. He saw several large chunks of ice bobbing up and down. Gradually he realized they were actually white whales. Now he understood what the guide had meant when he said that the Eskimos subsisted on white sea monsters. Trying in vain to curb his mounting excitement, Alexander saw that the portion of each whale appearing above the water was several times as large as the biggest of porpoises. These creatures, he estimated, must be at least thirty feet long.

The thought of capturing one, killing and dissecting it for scientific purposes was intoxicating. Not pausing to reflect on possible dangers, he shouted for the *voyageurs*, English Chief, and the guide. They launched his canoe and sped out across the open water in hot pursuit.

Not until they were paddling madly across the Arctic did Alexander realize that he had embarked on a wild, almost mad, enterprise. He and English Chief carried no weapons but their pistols and had no spare ammunition. The guide wore only a small skinning knife in his belt and the *voyageurs* were entirely unarmed.

It was dubious whether two pistol shots could kill even one of the monsters. And if one of the whales was attacked, the others in the school might assault the canoe itself.

Even so, Alexander was reluctant to abandon the chase. His curiosity was overpowering; then, too, he wanted to take back to the civilized world a complete report on the whales. At the same time, he realized that if he told his subordinates of his fears, he would lose their confidence.

So the wild race across the open sea went on, and gradually the fragile canoe drew closer to the whales. The nearest of them was soon no more than two hundred feet away. Alexander had no way of guessing whether the creatures realized men were near or whether they did not even care.

Drawing his pistol, he cocked it and prayed that his marksmanship would prove good. Then, unexpectedly, a fog rolled in across the sea, blanketing the whole area. Afraid that the canoe might strike one of the whales and be smashed to bits, Alexander ordered the *voyageurs* to turn back. But in the fog the men lost their sense of direction; they paddled aimlessly for more than an hour. Then around noon the fog cleared and a great iceberg loomed ahead.

Alexander wanted to climb onto the floating ice and explore it, but the fog closed in again, much to the relief of English Chief who had been ordered to accompany his leader.

Suddenly the sea became choppy. Sails were hoisted, but the swells were now so strong that Alexander, English Chief, and the guide were forced to bail steadily. Then, after another hour or more of paddling and bailing, the *voyageurs* guided the canoe back to the shore and the exhausted men were able to return to their camp.

Alexander commemorated the occasion by writing the name, Whale Island, on his map.

In the days that followed, the party explored the surrounding area but saw no Eskimos. Fish were plentiful but no game was found, and, with provisions dangerously low, Alexander finally decided, on July 16, to begin the return journey.

VII: THE GRIM VOYAGE

THE MEN WERE DELIGHTED when Alexander told them they would be going home. He was the only member of the party not heartily sick of the Arctic; the others wondered whether he had lost his mind when he said he would be pleased to spend a year in the region if he could obtain enough food.

Mosquitoes appeared in large swarms again; Alexander, however, had become impervious to their bites. Repeated stings had made him immune; instead of swelling, the tiny red dots disappeared now in a few minutes. The Indians became convinced that he possessed supernatural powers. They avoided him whenever possible.

Alexander was reluctant to leave when there was so much still to be seen. The party landed on an island used as an Eskimo graveyard and he insisted on spending the better part of an afternoon there. He was particularly fascinated by the large number of articles, such as wooden dishes and troughs, canoes and sleds, carried to the island to accommodate the spirits of the dead. The frames of the canoes were made entirely of whalebone; some parts were sewn with sinew, others were tied. The sledges were very sturdy and anywhere from four feet to eight feet long. Their bars extended more than two feet, their runners being two inches thick and approximately nine inches deep, while the skin prows, two and one-half feet high, were formed of two pieces sewn with whalebone.

The weather became pleasant again now and great numbers of wild-fowl were seen. After the hunters brought down several ducks and geese, the party looked forward to a dinner of something other than fish or pemmican. Alexander climbed a hill on the place he had named Graveyard Island to get a good view of the river. It was divided into innumerable streams that meandered through islands, some covered with wood, others with grass. The mountains on the far horizon appeared to be about forty miles away.

The food situation continued to improve. Two Chipewyans killed a pair of large reindeer. The meat was most welcome, for the pemmican had become moldy. There was fruit now, too; cranberries and pale-yellow raspberries grew in profusion in the valleys and lowlands near the river. Other edible plants flourished there as well, including sweet scallions and small, brown roots resembling potatoes which tasted better raw than cooked.

One night during a thunderstorm, the guide unexpectedly disappeared, leaving behind his precious moose skin. Evidently he was afraid of being taken south as a slave. He had been deeply impressed by the prowess of the white hunters who killed animals and birds at a great distance with their terrifying firearms.

The luck of the hunters remained good. Twenty-two geese were bagged; they were found to be delicious although considerably smaller than those on the Athabaska. Since they were molting and unable to fly, they were easy to catch. The next day an even more intensive hunt was conducted and forty more geese were shot. The problem of obtaining sufficient food was solved, at least for the immediate present.

But other equally grim troubles now presented themselves. On Tuesday, July 21, the canoes reached the head of the delta, one hundred miles from the mouth. When they entered the main stream, the current, its flow increased by melting ice and snow, was found to be very strong. Even the powerful and experienced *voyageurs* could make no headway.

So Alexander divided the entire party into two crews. One went ashore to tow the canoes up the river while the others rested. The labor was exhausting but necessary. Every day was precious if they hoped to reach Fort Chipewyan before the early winter closed in.

That night the party camped above the Narrows at the same spot where they had stayed on July 9. Shortly after the tents were erected, a party of Indians, led by the brother of the missing guide, arrived at the site. The brother, not being satisfied with Alexander's account of the guide's disappearance, made a long, angry speech. The *voyageurs*, alerted by Steinbruck, prepared for trouble.

The brother finally indicated that he would consider matters settled if he were given a string of red beads. But Mackenzie would not succumb to threats or blackmail, so he curtly refused the request. Instead, Alexander merely handed the warrior the bow and arrows the fugitive had left behind. At the same time, he made it plain that there would be no gifts.

To everyone's surprise, the Indians cheerfully accepted the terms. After that, they built their own fire, ate some fish they had with them, and then, to Alexander's astonishment, stripped naked to sleep. Curling up around the fire, they appeared to suffer no ill effects even though the night was bitterly cold.

When the march was resumed, the *voyageurs*, Red-Knives and Chipewyan again towed the heavily laden canoes and passengers. Tracking, as it was called, was back-breaking work, but there was no alternative.

The Indians traveled with the party and eventually arrived at the natives' principal settlement. Alexander seized this chance to trade. In return for a few beads, he obtained as many fish as the canoes could carry.

One trivial bit of information confirmed Mackenzie's belief that he had reached the Arctic. The Eskimos, his hosts told him, had seen some large boats on their sea eight or ten years earlier. Indeed, they had been close enough to the vessels to learn that the men on board were pale-skinned foreigners. Since that time they had called the Arctic Belhoulay Toe — or Pale Man's Lake. The natives were referring undoubtedly to the celebrated Arctic voyage of Captain James Cook, the most renowned naval explorer of the age.

For day after weary day now the men marched upstream, hauling the towlines. The Chipewyans and Red-Knives were so tired they insisted on calling frequent halts. Neither threats nor persuasion affected them. Alexander, wisely accepting the inevitable, suggested that the Indians go hunting. They did but returned empty-handed and disgruntled.

Alexander hid his own concern. In six days none of the provision stores had been touched. During that time, however, the company had consumed two reindeer, four swans, forty-five geese, and large quantities of fish. The leader knew that appetites were always sharp in the north, but in recent days they had soared far beyond his expectations. Actually his own appetite had become much keener, too. Obviously additional supplies would be needed sooner than he had anticipated.

An Indian, who was traveling from the direction of the mountains, fell in with the party now. When questioned about what lay to the west, he startled Alexander with information about another river beyond the mountains. It was, he said, stronger and far longer than the Mackenzie.

Only one little-known river fitted that description. Captain Cook has described a powerful body of water emptying into the Pacific, but he had been vague about its location. Alexander thought of this mighty stream as "Cook's River." Only many years later was it positively identified and named the Columbia River. Actually located far to the south, it forms the boundary between Oregon and Washington in the present-day United States.

This same Indian also graphically demonstrated his idea of the land to the west. Picking up a stick he drew a rough sketch in the sand on the river bank. He traced out a long point of land standing between two major rivers. Both of these streams fed into Pale Man's Lake, and at the far end of the lake stood a great *belhoulay couin* or a pale man's fort.

Alexander concluded that the brave was referring to Unalaska Fort, a trading post built in the Aleutian Islands by Russian hunters. Captain Cook had described the fort in detail in his report on the last of his voyages. Alexander had almost literally memorized that document.

He now assumed that the river to the west must be Cook's River, and that the body of water or sea — the Arctic — into which the Mackenzie discharged at Whale Island must be connected with Cook's River. If so, a roundabout but nevertheless feasible link with the Pacific could be located, since Cook's River was definitely believed to empty into the Pacific.

Alexander tried to get the brave to act as a guide and lead him to the river on the far side of the mountains. The man refused, then vanished. There was nothing to be done but continue the grueling march upstream.

Food was still difficult to find. With no fish in the river and game still scarce, the explorers had to open the last packages of parched corn. Everyone was hungry; tempers grew short.

English Chief became particularly hard to handle. Constantly in a foul mood, he spent hours speaking to no one even when addressed. Then, suddenly, he would fly into a fit of wild rage, and on several occasions the *voyageurs* had to restrain him for fear he would harm one of the other Indians or himself. He deeply resented the attentions paid to one of his squaws by a Chipewyan warrior. But far more upsetting to him was his ever-present fear that he would be forced to spend the winter wandering through the western mountains in search of a non-existent river. So he became almost completely uncooperative. On the rare occasions when isolated warriors were encountered, he either pretended ignorance of their language or gave evasive replies when Alexander pressed him for information.

On future expeditions of discovery, Alexander hoped to dispense with the services of an interpreter. That meant that in the interim he must master every possible Indian tongue.

But it was not easy to think in terms of the future now when so many urgent problems required immediate attention. The current of the river increased to eight to ten miles per hour; the winds, too, were favorable. Therefore, tracking had to be continued. The men towing the boats were forced to spend weary hours scrambling over rocks as they hauled the heavily laden canoes upstream.

On the night of August 1, the sky was dark enough for the stars to be seen. Alexander was able to plot his position much more accurately.

The following afternoon, seeing smoke ahead, he immediately quickened his pace, hopeful they were approaching a native bivouac. As he drew nearer to the smoke, however, a sulphurous odor became stronger and stronger.

76

Eventually he discovered that a fire was burning along a large part of the river bank.

Upon investigation they found that large deposits of coal extended from the surface to a great depth below the ground. The coals were burning slowly, giving off an intense heat. The small party could not extinguish the fire. Valuable coal was being wasted; both Alexander and Steinbruck felt helpless as they watched.

English Chief and the other natives were delighted. They ran along the beach gathering the softest chunks of coal they could find and refusing to continue the journey. Only then did Alexander learn that they considered coal a precious asset. They used it to blacken feathers and porcupine quills.

The weather was turning much colder now, even though some days were still warm and sunny. The nights were chilly, too; huge fires were built to protect the explorers from frostbite. Here and there beavers were shot; their fur was growing much longer. Obviously, winter would soon descend on the vast northwest territory. All possible speed was essential if they hoped to reach Fort Chipewyan before snow fell.

It was rarely possible now to paddle upstream; the current was swift and strong. The winds remained unfavorable too, so the canoes had to be hauled from early morning until late in the evening. The weary Indians, unable to think beyond the present, were inclined to dawdle. Alexander went ashore and helped them tow the boats. At no time now did he ride in the canoes. His physical endurance was inferior to that of the *voyageurs* and the natives, but he had no alternative. For hour after hour, day after day, he marched until his feet and legs, arms and hands became as tough as those of men who had spent all their adult lives in the wilderness.

From August 4 to August 10 the party could not use either sails or paddles. The men, working fifteen to eighteen hours each day, hauled the canoes and their cargo upstream. The river was no longer benign; at each turn, each bend, the water raced and churned with the speed of rapids. Frequently all the supplies and gear had to be unpacked and carried anywhere from a few feet to several hundred yards. Alexander wore out three pairs of moccasins; the others had the same trouble with their footgear.

One day when a moose was shot, the entire hide was used to make new moccasins. But these wore out even more rapidly, for the men had had no opportunity to cure the leather slowly.

The thought that the mountains would be left behind soon disturbed Alexander greatly. He felt that if he could only climb to the summit of one of the higher peaks, he might catch a glimpse of the river or rivers on the far side.

A young warrior of an unknown tribe, encountered on the morning of August 11, claimed to know the mountains well. He agreed to take Alexander to the top of one of the great peaks in return for a gift of a pistol, ammunition, and gunpowder.

So now, while the rest of the party took their ease, Alexander set out with his guide. They marched overland, setting a rapid pace, but soon came to a forest difficult to penetrate because the summer growth was so luxurious. Branches, vines, and underbrush appeared everywhere; Alexander's buckskins were ripped, but he pressed forward. Eventually he and the guide emerged from the woods. They were disappointed to see that the mountains, visible again, seemed just as far off as they had from the bank of the river.

As they made their way upward across a plateau, Alexander's hopes rose momentarily, then fell again when they were forced to struggle through a muddy, mosquito-infested, seemingly endless swamp. At seven o'clock in the evening they were still in the marsh, so the pair reluctantly abandoned the journey and returned to the bivouac on the Mackenzie. Two and one-half hours later, the march was resumed.

The Chipewyan hunters told Alexander that in the meantime they had encountered several parties of local natives in the forest. So he immediately ordered English Chief both to find the natives and to ask them about the land to the west. When the Chipewyan was slow in obeying, one of the Red-Knives warned the leader that English Chief and his wives were so afraid of being forced to spend another full year in the wilderness that they intended to desert at the first opportunity.

The Red-Knife said, too, that he believed English Chief had learned more about the region on the far side of the mountain range than he had communicated to his superior. Apparently that report caused Alexander to abandon all plans of returning to Fort Chipewyan, and he at once confronted English Chief with the charges. The Indian weakly denied them. A serious crisis was now brewing.

Alexander was bitterly disappointed. His mood did not improve, either, two days later when packages of pemmican buried on the journey north were removed from the earth and proved to be moldy. Though he did not realize it at the moment, his own nerves were raw. A seemingly minor incident precipitated the crisis.

The party came unexpectedly upon an Indian camp. The natives fled, however, when they caught sight of the explorers, and Alexander sent his Chipewyan ahead to explain that he meant no harm and that he was willing to pay handsomely for information about the country to the west.

But when he reached the camp site on a hillside beside the river, he found English Chief dividing the property left behind by the frightened Indians. The sight infuriated him. He completely lost his temper. Everyone — including Steinbruck, Bishop, and the *voyageurs* — was ordered to search the forest for the missing Indians. English Chief was so slow in leaving that Alexander's fury mounted. He called the Chipewyan a lazy thief, accused him of deliberately sabotaging the expedition, and blamed him for their failures.

However, no sign of the fugitives was found, so what might have been the leader's last hope of obtaining information about the land to the west had vanished with them.

English Chief brooded over his loss of face. After camp was made for the night, he came to Alexander to denounce him angrily. The moment for a final showdown had come.

Alexander held his emotions in check now, but refused to spare the Indian's feelings. Summoning his entire company, he made a short, curt speech. English Chief, he said, had failed all of them. They had traveled a long distance at great expense. They had suffered many hardships and were very tired. All their efforts had been in vain because of one man's stupid, stubborn refusal to obey orders English Chief replied in a hysterical speech, concluding by shouting that he would accompany the expedition no farther. The other Chipewyan said they would leave the party too. Then, simulating grief, they prostrated themselves on the ground, wailed and beat each other on the head and shoulders.

Alexander let them work themselves into a state of emotional exhaustion. He was wise now in the ways of Indians and made no attempt to stem their hysteria. He still needed them, but he also realized that it would be very difficult for them to reach their own land without him. At last when they grew calmer, Alexander invited English Chief to dine with him privately that evening. After the offer was accepted, the Indian interpreter was given two drams of rum which soothed his ruffled feelings. He confessed, however, that, having shed tears, he must obey the custom of his people by taking to the warpath the following spring to wipe away the shame of behaving like a woman. Then he discussed the possible enemies he might attack.

For the present, at any rate, his melancholy had vanished; he promised faithfully to remain with the party as long as he was needed. When he and Alexander parted for the night, the leader gave the Chipewyan several drams of rum to take with him. The liquor would prevent a relapse.

The incident was closed. Unfortunately it did not alter the basic situation. Alexander still had not obtained the information he wanted so desperately and, barring an unexpected development, he would probably learn nothing of real value about the land to the west.

VIII: THE HOMECOMING

IN THE LAST DAYS of the homeward journey, unexpected dangers plagued the weary explorers. The food shortage remained critical and their problems were aggravated by rains and heavy winds. When the party reached Great Slave Lake, the winds were still so violent that they were compelled to curtail the voyage, make camp, and stay there for two days and nights.

It was urgently necessary to obtain food now at whatever the cost in time and energy. Alexander decided to head for the hut built by Laurent LeRoux on the north arm of the lake. It would have been shorter to sail straight for the southern shore, but he had no choice.

The voyage undertaken the following day was the most hazardous of the entire journey. The party was sailing off an exposed shore, the water was shallow and filled with half-hidden boulders. Two men in Alexander's canoe worked constantly to bail out the water that leaked into the craft on all sides; the wind was so fierce that the sail might be carried away at any moment. But in spite of the dangers, they made good progress. That night the men were so exhausted that they did not even bother to erect their tents; they just rolled themselves in their blankets and went to sleep before an open fire.

Alexander roused the party early the next morning and the voyage was resumed. At four o'clock that afternoon, three canoes appeared in the distance, all carrying sails. The two parties met on the water. So Alexander was reunited with LeRoux. The clerk was accompanied by a family of Indians; they had gone with him on a trading and hunting expedition.

The hunting unfortunately had been poor, so Alexander's food shortage was not relieved. But the canoes were filled with bales of prime marten skins that would bring high prices in the Montreal market. Montreal, however, was far away, and trouble continued to plague the augmented party.

English Chief's canoe was smashed on a boulder near the shore and the Chipewyan were fortunate to escape with their lives. Rations of whisky were issued to all hands. But even then, it was difficult for them to remain cheerful because the storm grew worse. Violent winds tore down trees, making travel of any kind out of the question. For two days and two nights the party could not move.

When the weather finally improved a little, English Chief announced that he and his people were leaving at once to spend the winter with their relatives, the Beaver Indians. Alexander said good-by to them, and the torturous journey was resumed. The wind increased again, forcing an early landing. The *voyageurs* set out nets, but dinner that evening consisted of the last of LeRoux' pemmican and parched corn.

There was no sleep that night because the gale became worse and worse. When a tent was blown down, the men could not raise it again. The water of the lake was still so turbulent that LeRoux advised against trying to resume the voyage and Alexander reluctantly agreed with him. The weather turned bitterly cold; everyone knew that the early autumn of the north had come.

But there was one cheering note next morning. The nets were filled with fish! The party ate a hearty breakfast, the largest meal consumed in days. Afterward Steinbruck, Bishop, the Red-Knives, and the *voyageurs* went hunting.

In the early evening two shots were heard across the bay; shortly thereafter a large fire was seen. Alexander ordered his own campfire built higher to indicate his party's position.

Later that night English Chief suddenly appeared at the bivouac. He was drenched to the skin and reported that his people's last boat had been smashed, their kettles and supplies lost. The other Chipewyan soon followed in his wake. All of them were in a bedraggled state, happy to accept the clothing Alexander donated out of his own baggage.

In the morning the men marched along the shore of the north arm; they finally reached LeRoux' hut. The clerk's food stocks there were plentiful, so everybody, for the first time in months, enjoyed moose steak, elk chops, and bear bacon.

When the Chipewyan staggered into the post late in the day, Alexander gave them plentiful supplies of tobacco, ironware, and ammunition, and arranged for English Chief to bring the Beaver Indians to the post to trade that winter. Promised a liberal reward in return for his efforts, the interpreter swore that he would see that his relatives would appear, armed with many bales of fur.

Alexander, accompanied by Steinbruck, Bishop, and the *voyageurs*, took their leave of LeRoux the following day. Great flocks of geese, ducks, cranes, and swans were constantly overhead now, flying south. The men shot down enough birds to satisfy their wants for some days. But the birds seemed to be in a panicky state and Alexander knew that snow and frost would come at any time; the heavy clouds of wild fowl overhead spurred the men to greater efforts. They sailed when possible, paddled as long as they could, and portaged when necessary.

The last days on the trail were arduous. The weather was foul and grew steadily worse, but at least the party was well fed.

Finally, on a cold, blustery afternoon, they reached Fort Chipewyan. The explorers were greeted warmly, and the weary travelers took hot baths, ate dinner, and went straight to bed.

Alexander Mackenzie was not sleepy, however; he retired to a private room with his notebooks. There he summed up the accomplishments and failures of his round-trip journey of one hundred and two days. He had not found the northwest passage across the continent to the Pacific; he was bitterly disappointed because he had failed to win the prize of twenty thousand pounds sterling offered by the British government for that feat.

Nevertheless, he had found a hitherto unknown major river and had traveled fifteen hundred miles up its waters to its outlet in the Arctic. He had opened a territory of approximately seven hundred and fifty thousand square miles, staking the claim of the North-West Company to a region believed to be rich in fur-bearing animals.

His notebooks and maps would aid men who followed him into the area; his scientific observation would be eagerly studied by scholars at all of the world's great universities. Yet, in spite of all this, Alexander Mackenzie was not satisfied; he was more determined than ever to find the northwest passage. In the meantime, there was much to be done.

On the very day that he reached the fort, he began a long report to his partners in Montreal. Two days later, a junior clerk started off on the long journey to Montreal, carrying the letter, a hastily drawn map of the area discovered, and an appraisal of the fur-trading potentials of the region. Then, while the details of the journey remained fresh in his mind, Alexander sat down to prepare a final version of the *Journal* he intended to publish. He also worked long and hard on the maps of the Northwest Territory, his furious energy compensating for his lack of skill as a cartographer.

Steinbruck, meantime, returned to civilization and began to sing the praises of the diminutive Scotsman who had accomplished so much in such a short time.

Alexander had leisure now to plan his future. As he sat before the fire at Fort Chipewyan, he came to several resolutions. First of all, he knew too little of astronomy and navigation to make accurate observations. Furthermore, he did not own the right equipment for that purpose. Therefore, he concluded, he must go to England to pursue studies enabling him to pinpoint a journey to the Pacific with precision.

His equipment on the Arctic trip had been inadequate, too. Now he spent a portion of the winter designing tools and canoes better suited to his rugged purposes. The tents carried on his expedition had been a nuisance, so he decided that on future expeditions he would use sleeping bags. They would be far more convenient, less bulky and infinitely easier to handle.

In the early spring of 1790 when the thaws came, he left Fort Chipewyan and covered the eighteen hundred and fifty miles to Grand Portage in two months.

His reception at Grand Portage was a foretaste of what awaited him at Montreal. Senior and junior clerks showed their awe of him, as did the *voyageurs* gathered there. But two of his partners in the North-West Company greeted him coolly. Making no mention of his discoveries, they confined their discussions to the fur-trading potential of the country he had opened. Mackenzie shrugged off their hostility and left a few days later for Montreal.

Scores of *voyageurs* in canoes and bateaux came down the St. Lawrence to greet him at Lachine and escort him in triumph to Montreal. There a huge crowd of three or four thousand persons hailed him. Alexander had to make the first speech of his life. After stammering his thanks, he said he had been very fortunate and that he wished everyone well.

His cousin, Roderic, was waiting, too, and joined him in his old lodgings. They ate dinner together in privacy. No North-West partners came to call. Roderic explained that his older cousin was expected to attend a board meeting the following day. The tight-lipped Alexander merely nodded. Over coffee he announced that he intended to use his increased power to obtain a full partnership for Roderic.

That same evening a mysterious, smiling gentleman armed with letters of introduction came to see Alexander. They went into a long, secret conference behind closed doors. Both were smiling when they parted.

The following morning, the partners of North-West met formally. Simon McTavish greeted Alexander with a brief handshake; the others were equally distant. Alexander listened to them in silence as they discussed the financial aspects of his discoveries. Then, suddenly, he seized the offensive. The income of the company, he said, would be doubled; he demanded a larger share of the profits. Mackenzie was voted the increase unanimously. Then, too, Roderic's promotion was voted quickly.

Every man in the room knew that the influence of the old guard had been reduced; the real power had been transferred to a slender young man with a sun-tanned face and calloused hands. The company's domain had been doubled, thanks to Alexander's discoveries, so he could demand whatever he wanted. And this, he knew.

The conservative, middle-aged partners were uneasy; by banding together they hoped to keep him in line. McTavish and the other seniors, now in their sixties and seventies, tried to conceal their alarm. Once they, too, had been radical, but since then their policies and methods had made them wealthy. They had no intention of letting a young upstart dictate to them.

Alexander thought he was prepared to cope with his partners' hostility, but the canny McTavish struck first. It had come to his attention, he said, that Mackenzie had entertained a visitor the previous evening.

Alexander nodded calmly.

Was it true, McTavish went on, that the guest had been an employee of the rival Hudson's Bay Company?

No, Alexander replied, the man was not a hireling; he was a principal shareholder empowered to speak on behalf of his colleagues. The gentleman had proposed that Hudson's Bay, still the larger concern, merge with North-West.

The men in the board room were horrified. After all, they had formed North-West to compete with Hudson's Bay.

Alexander added quietly that he was in complete agreement with the plan to merge with their great rival.

McTavish appeared stunned.

The elderly, conservative MacLeod begged Alexander to remember that, Roderic excepted, he was North-West's youngest partner. It ill became him to even suggest such a consolidation, for he simply did not know what was at stake.

Alexander now began to cite figures. He anticipated that in the next ten years North-West would increase the volume of its business by more than one hundred per cent. And if the fur markets remained steady, profits should quadruple in that time. A merger, however, would permit a pooling of resources with Hudson's Bay and the business potential would be much greater: the volume of trade would go up by more than two hundred and twenty per cent, and profits would increase nine-fold.

McTavish interrupted testily. Figures were meaningless, he declared. What's more, there would be no merger as long as he remained chairman of the board.

Alexander stood and said flatly that he intended to use all his influence to consolidate the two companies. Then, leaving his partners gasping, he walked out of the meeting.

The news of his stand created a sensation throughout the business world. Investors everywhere said his position was sound. North-West had become almost as big as Hudson's Bay. The two giants would ruin each other if they fought a no-holds-barred commercial war. In London and Liverpool and Manchester, New York and Boston and Philadelphia, Alexander was hailed as a financial genius.

But the pedlars in Montreal sourly branded him a traitor.

He declared, in response, that a merger of the two companies was inevitable. He said he was willing to wait, however, until his partners came to their senses. They replied by trying to buy him out, but he insisted that they didn't have money enough to do so.

The feud was then shunted aside. In succeeding months Alexander worked with his partners to exploit to the full the territory he had opened. Pending a merger, Hudson's Bay was still North-West's rival, and, as Alexander knew the vast area he had found, better than anyone else, he alone was in a position to direct the senior and junior clerks now sent in large numbers into the Mackenzie River basin to trade with the Indians. Displaying the same drive shown on his own expedition, Alexander worked eighteen to twenty hours per day.

Late in the summer of 1790, he decided his presence was needed in person at Fort Chipewyan. He reached the settlement on Lake Athabaska before snow fell. Spending the entire winter there, he supervised preparations for fur-trading on a mammoth scale, and in the spring he dispatched more than twenty fur expeditions.

Then he himself traveled the long eighteen hundred and fifty miles back to Grand Portage and went on to Montreal. A few of North-West's partners now agreed with him about merging with Hudson's Bay. Simon McTavish was still hostile, however, and hesitated when Alexander applied for a one-year leave of absence. Before McTavish could reply, the young man declared that, of course, he did not intend to deal with Hudson's Bay during that time. He then explained that he wanted to devote a year to purely private matters. The leave of absence was granted.

Alexander sat down and wrote a jubilant letter to Roderic at far-off Fort Chipewyan, saying that at last he was finally to be able to pursue his aim of finding a northwest passage to the Pacific.

IX: GOLD AND GLORY: PREPARATION FOR ADVENTURE

ALEXANDER, now twenty-six years old, traveled incognito to England. He created no attention whatsoever when he took inexpensive rooms in London. After spending several weeks buying books and scientific instruments, he went to Cambridge to enroll at that great university. There he took courses in astronomy, navigation, mathematics, and geography.

He spent the entire autumn and winter in Cambridge, just one of many hundreds of anonymous students. He was, to be sure, six to eight years older than the majority of undergraduates, but fortunately no one thought this odd. Others in their twenties, many of them fellow Scotsmen, had been forced to work for several years to finance a higher education. So Alexander was accepted as one of this group, his Scottish burr standing him in good stead.

His achievements in the New World were well known, of course, but because he was enrolled under an assumed name virtually no one at the university was familiar with his personal background. The dons, fellows, and other faculty members probably thought him unusually earnest, but Cambridge had always attracted serious students. And the undergraduates, with whom he had so little in common, found him taciturn and boring. They made no attempt to force their company on him.

University life, as such, did not interest him. His sole aim was to absorb as much knowledge as possible in a short time. The few undergraduates who became acquainted with him — yet did not know his true identity — were astonished by his energy. He lived as he had on his journey to the Arctic; he thought nothing of working eighteen or twenty hours a day, seven days a week.

When the winter term ended at Easter, he returned to London. There he immediately wrote a letter to Roderic, ordering his cousin to send men up the Peace River to cut large quantities of lumber for a new fort. His long-range plans for discovering a northwest passage had jelled in his mind.

Remaining in London for approximately two months, he spent most of his time at the coffee houses frequented by merchants in the fur trade. From them he learned of their wants; several with whom he became friendly showed him the kind of beaver and marten and seal skins they liked best. He even ate a number of meals with men in the employ of the North-West Company without telling them that he was their superior.

Finally, before sailing for Montreal, he went to the London waterfront in search of seamen who had sailed with Captain Cook on his voyage along the Pacific coast. Finding two such, he paid them to answer numerous questions about all they had seen in the New World.

Alexander was now in the best possible position to win both glory and the financial reward offered by the British government for the discovery of a northwest passage. His partnership in North-West already gave him an assured annual income of at least four thousand pounds — perhaps thirty-five thousand dollars a year in modern terms. Then, too, his previous journey had given him experience no other explorer could boast. And now he had rounded off his education at Cambridge and in London.

Alexander spent four weeks crossing the Atlantic, but he was busy most of the time. He devoted his days to reading histories, diaries, and journals of previous explorers, and every evening he carried his instruments to the deck and practiced with them. After the captain of the merchantman became curious about the strange passenger who plotted their course so assiduously, Alexander confided his identity but swore the skipper to secrecy. Thereafter he shot the stars nightly from the quarterdeck, isolated from the other passengers who were inclined to be too curious and talkative.

The books he read put his own search for the northwest passage in proper perspective; from them he learned more than he had thought possible about the hazards awaiting him. Most of all, he confirmed his own belief that he would need courage and stamina to meet the test ahead.

Spain, as Mackenzie already knew, had been on the Pacific since Balboa first discovered that ocean in 1513, and there were small Spanish settlements in the Pacific coast area known as the Californias where most of the Spanish residents were missionaries. But the vast deserts standing between settlements in Mexico and the area to the north had prevented large-scale migration. Apparently no determined attempt had been made to explore the area to the north until the eighteenth century.

The most significant discoveries in the Pacific northwest had been made by Vitus Bering, a Danish sea captain and explorer in the employ of the Russians. The stations set up by the Russians in the Aleutians and along the northernmost shores of North America in the region called Unalaska were a direct outgrowth of Bering's discoveries. As a consequence, Russian traders held a world-wide monopoly in the sea-otter trade.

Spain, attracted by the commercial possibilities, belatedly entered the race. By 1778, when Captain Cook first landed on the shores of the Californias, Spain had established posts at Monterey, San Diego, and San Francisco.

Cook, a methodical man, put into many bays along the Pacific coast, entering — among others — gulfs in Prince William Sound and the stream he discovered and gave his name to — Cook's River. Most of the natives encountered by Cook had never before seen civilized men.

An American sea captain named John Meares, sailing in a small ship named the *Washington*, reported that he had found an inland sea east of Vancouver Island. Alexander carried a copy of Meares' account with him on board the merchantman. If Meares was right, the inland sea might be the outlet of a river that crossed the mountains. Here, perhaps, was the northwest passage. In any event, Alexander was convinced that a river crossed the Rocky Mountains from British territory to the Pacific. His plans were laid accordingly.

This time he spent only a few days at Montreal. Because the territory in the northwest was already yielding such large quantities of furs, his partners had decided to hold their annual meeting at Grand Portage rather than at Montreal. He accompanied them on the now familiar journey to Lake Superior; later, after the meeting, he left them to make the eighteen hundred and fifty mile trip to Fort Chipewyan.

There he and Roderic began to prepare for the new journey of exploration. And now the British government, caught up in the fever of the race to find an overland route to the Pacific, increased its reward to thirty thousand pounds.

On this trip Alexander was leaving nothing to chance. He carried with him large quantities of the equipment and trading merchandise he believed, from previous experience, he would need. For trading purposes he had acquired:

Coarse woolen blankets of various sizes
Small arms
Muskets

Ammunition

Gunpowder

Tobacco

Cotton goods made in Manchester and brought with him across the Atlantic

Linens and coarse sheetings

Thread

Lines

Twine

Common hardware

Cutlery and ironmongery of several descriptions

Kettles of brass and copper

Kettles of sheet-iron

Silk and cotton handkerchiefs

Hats, shoes, and hose

Beads

He also carried equipment for his *voyageurs*. For each man he had two fine English blankets, two shirts, two pairs of trousers, and two pairs of stout boots waterproofed in oil. He also took with him a large quantity of the tobacco that the *voyageurs* loved. Each of the rifles had been tested for dependability, and his knives were made of the best Sheffield steel. Packed with his gear were barrels of hardtack or biscuits, as well as hogsheads of salt pork and sacks of peas. These supplies would last for a long time without spoiling. Roderic had also prepared pemmican and parched corn for him. Alexander knew, however, that the men became sulky and listless on a monotonous diet. He would now be able to vary it.

His oilcloths were lightweight, and his sails were made of the best canvas to be found in England. His towing lines were thin but unusually strong. He carried only two kettles for his party to use in the field, because he had burdened himself unnecessarily with more on the trip to the Arctic. Gum and bark for repairing boats had been selected with great care; he carried the best variety of *watape*, made of divided roots of spruce fir. It would swell when wet and render a canoe waterproof.

His supplies included rum, whisky, and brandy, too, but he told no one how much liquor he carried. The *voyageurs* were always inclined to drink too much when given the opportunity. Indians, too, were invariably anxious to sample strong spirits. So the liquor was stored away with his own personal effects.

Two important members of the expedition were waiting for Alexander at Chipewyan. One was Bishop, advanced now to the rank of junior clerk with the North-West Company. As a veteran of the journey to the Arctic, he thoroughly understood Alexander's ways.

The other was a brilliant, hard-bitten, young senior clerk, Alexander Mackay. A Scotsman by birth, he had made a lasting impression on Mackenzie when they had met for the first time in Montreal the previous year. He surpassed other applicants for the position of second-in-command both temperamentally and physically. A giant who towered above the diminutive leader of the expedition, he had earned a reputation for fearlessness. Mackay was energetic, imaginative, and fully as eager as his superior to find the northwest passage.

Shortly before leaving Fort Chipewyan, Alexander wrote a letter to McTavish, urging that North-West reconsider its opposition to a merger with the Hudson's Bay Company. It was the last communication he sent to his partners before taking off.

On the morning of October 10, 1792, Alexander set out from Fort Chipewyan, accompanied by Mackay, Bishop, and six *voyageurs*, all men who had been selected for their physical stamina, intelligence, and eagerness to join the attack on the wilderness. They traveled in two canoes, both heavily laden with equipment, food, and articles for trading with Indians they might encounter.

Winter was fast approaching. Alexander was in a great hurry; he had to establish his advance base camp before snow and ice made the task impossible. He intended to build a camp on the Peace River, running on a course almost due west from Lake Athabaska. Remaining at that camp for the winter, he would start from there when the weather became warm enough the following spring. His chances of success would be better if he made his final take-off from a place as far west as possible. His party was followed by some of Roderic's men in two other canoes, carrying supplies for the winter.

On November 1, the members of the expedition finally reached the spot on the riverbank that Alexander had selected for his winter camp. Seventy Indians were on hand to bid him welcome, but they displayed signs of anxiety. Alexander, knowing that he would have to live near them until spring, presented each with four inches of twist tobacco. He also gave every warrior the equivalent of one dram of rum, at the same time admonishing the chief of the tribe to see that the liquor was used with discretion.

After making these gifts, Alexander warned the chief that in the months ahead he expected the natives to co-operate. If they tried to steal any of his property, he said, he would punish them severely. But if they behaved honestly, they could expect from him the greatest kindness and consideration.

Not one building was ready yet, but the two men sent out by Roderic the previous spring had been diligent in cutting wood. So enough planks to build a large house were available. Many difficulties hampered the group, however. The ground was frozen hard, and the frost was so severe that the axes of the workmen became as brittle as glass.

The hardships suffered by the two woodsmen had been intense. They had lived for months in a shelter made of underbrush, but they were still in good condition and displayed high spirits. All the members of the expedition joined them now in building the house and storage sheds. And even though the travelers were exhausted after their strenuous journey from Fort Chipewyan, there was no time to lose. A heavy snowfall, due at any time, would hamper their work and prolong their suffering in the intense cold.

In the meantime Alexander concentrated upon providing a steady supply of winter food. As always, provisions were his main concern; he was reluctant to dip into the stores brought with him. After conferring, through the Beaver interpreter, with the chief of the local tribe, he arranged for the services of four hunters familiar with the use of firearms.

Progress on the building of the house was slow, painfully slow. The men could not move indoors until the end of November. Then they celebrated the completion of their winter home by spending a full day before a blazing fire in the stone hearth. That night, too, everyone slept around the fire.

The weather was so cold that, on December 2, Alexander's only Fahrenheit thermometer broke. Thereafter he could not record the temperature. He realized once again that man was at the mercy of the elements. He felt helpless, particularly since so many men were depending on him. But he kept himself busy so that he wouldn't brood.

One morning a *voyageur*, working on a section of the roof of the house, came to the leader complaining of a pain in his arm. Alexander found a swollen red stripe about one-half inch wide extending from the patient's thumb to his shoulder. The amateur physician had no idea how to treat the malady, but he wanted at least to set the man's mind at rest. So, mixing some rum and soap into a volatile linament, he ordered the concoction spread on the red portion of his patient's body.

The *voyageur* obtained no immediate relief. Blotches of red gradually covered his entire face and body. That night he went out of his mind, raving, cursing, and weeping.

Alexander consulted his medical books in vain. He could not diagnose the man's ailment, much less remedy it. Under the circumstances, he decided to do nothing. Perhaps the man would improve by morning. The *voyageur*, still shouting, was put to bed and, after a time, he became quiet.

The others drifted off to bed, too, and at first no sound was heard but the hissing of fires in the hearths. Then, suddenly, a wild shriek echoed through the rooms. Another *voyageur* raced to Alexander with the news that the patient had run amok.

The leader found the sick man standing in one of the uncompleted rooms, hacking wildly at an outside wall with a double-edged axe. Several men were trying to reason with him, but he paid them no attention. Apparently he was too far gone to hear.

Alexander ordered the *voyageur* to drop the axe. The man completely ignored him. There was now no choice but to take the axe from him. Alexander stepped forward boldly. The man turned, shouting incoherently, his eyes bright, and started to raise the heavy weapon over his head. Plainly the *voyageur* intended to attack his leader.

Leaping forward, Alexander wrenched the axe from the *voyageur's* hand and, even though the man towered above him, struck the patient with such force that he dropped to the floor. Others pounced on him, too, tying his hands and feet and carrying him back to his bed.

Something had to be done to relieve the man's suffering. Alexander decided to bleed him, a common cure-all in the eighteenth century. Even though he had never performed this operation, he could not afford to let that deter him now.

Not daring to expose the *voyageur* to the freezing outdoor weather, he decided to perform the operation before the largest hearth in the unfinished house. A howling wind, seeping through the chinks between the planks of wood, added to the tension. At times the gusts were so strong, even inside the structure, that candles were blown out.

Alexander sent one of the men for an oil lamp, heated a skinning knife in the hearth and then wiped it with brandy. With three strong men pinning him to a table of rough wood, the patient was bled.

Thereafter the *voyageur* slept soundly. When he opened his eyes around eight in the morning, he was rational. He had no recollection of his insane behavior of the night before. Declaring he was ravenous, he demanded breakfast. Given a large buffalo steak, he consumed every bit of it. His rash began to fade now; the crisis was ended. In the days that followed, his rash gradually disappeared altogether, and in two weeks he resumed his full share of the work load.

No other violence disturbed the peace of the cold winter. The house was completed, a palisade was built, and all the trading goods, equipment, and provisions were moved inside the compound. Thereafter it was not necessary to maintain so sharp a watch on the property.

Late in the winter, Alexander learned that two warriors from a tribe somewhere to the west were visiting the nearby Indian village. He immediately asked them to visit him. When he found he could not understand their language, he summoned his Beaver interpreter.

What the braves told Alexander excited him greatly. The local Indians, they said, called themselves a Rocky Mountain nation but had no right to the name. They themselves were real Rocky Mountain Indians, living in the shadow of the great peaks. Claiming to be familiar with the mountains, they said they could navigate the rivers that roared down into the plains from the heights.

Alexander promptly engaged them to remain with him now and to act as guides for his company when he set out to cross the mountains. Unfortunately, the Indians had never been on the far side of the mountains. It was strange, Alexander thought, that the idea of making their way down the far side of the peaks had never occurred to them.

In any event, they assured him that the countryside between the compound and the mountains was fertile and easy to cross. Buffalo were plentiful on the plains; deer, caribou, and elk could be found in the forests. Hunting was always good; only a few small tribes of Indians lived beneath the mountains and they rarely competed for food. The rivers and lakes were well stocked with whitefish, trout, and several other kinds of fish whose names could not be translated into English.

Travel occasionally became difficult, the Rocky Mountain warriors warned, because there were many rapids in the rivers. But beavers by the thousands abounded on the shores of the streams. Alexander, mindful that he was also a trader, was intrigued as the Indians described in detail where beaver furs could be obtained.

Finally, the braves claimed to have met men from the other side of the mountains who had told them of a great and powerful river that flowed to a huge sea. Alexander had no reason to think that the natives might be exaggerating or lying. They became somewhat confused, however, when they tried to describe the course of the river. One said it flowed toward the southwest; the other insisted it ran toward the northwest. The latter believed the course very difficult.

Alexander wondered whether they might be talking about two branches of a single river. If so, the southern fork might be more easily navigated.

The Indians agreed the distance across the Continental Divide, as this is now known, was short. When questioned about their own lack of interest in what lay on the other side of the peaks, they merely shrugged. The Beaver interpreter explained that the tribes living on the near side of the mountains lived such an easy life that they had no compelling reason to go exploring.

That night Alexander could not sleep. Leaving his warm bed, he went out into the open and stood for a long time staring at the Peace River which would lead him toward the west. Although the night was cold, a faint, almost elusive hint of spring was in the air. Very soon now he would embark on the greatest adventure of his life.

X: THE GREAT ADVENTURE

WITH THE COMING of warmer weather, the solid sheet of ice on the surface of the Peace River began to melt. Final preparations for the great adventure were speeded.

Alexander had spent the entire winter worrying about transportation. He had finally decided to use just one large canoe. Built to his specifications, it was so light that two men could carry it for a distance of three or four miles without halting. The craft was twenty-five feet long on the inside exclusive of curves at prow and stern, twenty-six inches deep, and four feet, nine inches wide.

The canoe contained many ribs; it was large enough to carry the party's entire cargo of provisions, trading goods, gifts, arms and ammunition, baggage and emergency equipment. In addition, every member of the expedition could ride in it. Alexander reasoned that if they had only one canoe to carry over portages, the party would make far better time than if they traveled in several smaller craft.

Mackay was now officially designated the second-in-command of the expedition. Bishop had no title and no authority; he wanted none, considering himself lucky just to be included. There were six *voyageurs* in the group, all eager volunteers, all powerful giants selected for their physical prowess, amiability, and endurance. Two had been members of the earlier Arctic expedition. The two Rocky Mountain Indians retained by Alexander during the winter completed the party. They would act as guides, interpreters, and hunters.

On May 8 the men were feverishly busy making last-minute preparations. Baggage, equipment, and trading goods were carefully inspected. Firearms and gunpowder were checked. Mackay looked closely at all the food supplies, but Alexander, taking no chances, examined every ninety-pound piece himself. He packed his own scientific gear; no one else was allowed to touch it. The *voyageurs* checked every seam in the canoe. Bishop listed the luggage and supervised the storing of the cargo in the boat.

Finally, late in the afternoon of May 9, everything was ready. Alexander rejoiced because he was leaving a month earlier than he had planned, thus assuring, he hoped, ample time to make the journey and return before winter.

The men now sat down to their last meal at a table, gorging themselves on roasted venison and buffalo steaks, turnips and tiny delicious squash from the Indian village. Each man ate several whitefish, and Alexander poured festive cups of wine, making certain, however, that the *voyageurs* and Indians did not drink too much.

The meal lasted for a long time; the men did not rise from the table until six o'clock in the evening. Everyone expected the journey to begin the following morning, but Alexander had a surprise in store. They would leave at once, he said, in accordance with the custom of traders who always started on a voyage in the early evening.

Knives were hastily sharpened, and the men's firearms were cleaned, checked, and loaded. Then the entire group gathered in the living room of the house where a prayer was offered for their safe return. Next the voyageurs carried the canoe down to the water and launched it. Mackay and Bishop joined them, and the Beaver interpreter dissolved in tears.

Promptly at seven o'clock, Alexander arrived, carrying his precious telescope and notebooks. After he took his seat in the prow of the canoe, Mackay barked an order. The *voyageurs* dipped their paddles into the waters of the Peace River.

The great journey had begun.

The river was rising, and the current flowing toward the east was strong so from the very start the oarsmen had a difficult time.

Alexander deliberately left to Mackay the task of supervising most details of the *voyageurs'* work. When, for example, camp was made for the night, Mackay directed the raising of the tents. On his first journey, the leader had been forced to spend too much of his own time directing routine operations. So now he had chosen Mackay as his lieutenant. The clerk proved to be a forceful, exceptionally capable man.

The canoe was less trustworthy. The following morning it began to leak. The heavy load was responsible. Mackay ordered a landing made. The boat was patched with gum, then the voyage was resumed.

The ground rose now at intervals to considerable heights; at every pause in the rise there was a gently ascending area. The grass was so thick and even that it reminded Alexander of a lawn.

The entire "theater of Nature," as he called it, was dotted with thick groves of poplar and spruce. And everywhere one saw vast herds of elk and buffalo. The former preferred the uplands; the buffalo, whose young frisked about them, abounded on the plains. In fact, the area was so crowded with wild animals that, in places, it reminded Alexander of a stall-yard.

A few days later they spotted two enormous grizzly bears in the distance; the guides confessed their fear of the beasts. Members of their tribe never attacked a bear unless the hunting party boasted at least four warriors.

The nervousness of the Indians became greater as the day passed, for the tracks of many grizzlies were seen. Then on an island the explorers discovered the *watee* — or den — of a huge bear. Alexander measured it, the den was ten feet long, five feet high, and six feet wide.

White birch trees now appeared in abundance, and the party paused long enough to gather bark for future patching of the canoe. It still had to be gummed every night. Alexander began to wish he had used two smaller boats. Game was still plentiful; huge herds of buffalo still cavorted and stamped on the plains, and the hunters, going off to the distant hills in the north each evening, always returned with elk.

Then, rounding a bend in the river on Friday, May 17, they saw the Rocky Mountains in the distance, their peaks covered with snow. Alexander was delighted; he had not expected to reach them so soon. He estimated that they were now approximately eighty to one hundred miles away, but could not be certain because his telescope and other instruments were of little use in judging distance. His excitement increased, however, when the river narrowed to a width of about one hundred yards; high bluffs, appearing on either side, cut off the party's view of the plains beyond. One such bluff was more than two thousand feet high.

Alexander wondered now if they might reach the mountains more quickly than they had hoped. The Indians warned him, however, that dangerous rapids were said to be ahead. But Alexander, recalling his over-cautious approach to the little falls when sailing down the Mackenzie River, waved aside their advice. Indians, he had found, almost always exaggerated and usually did not realize when they were distorting the truth.

A small party of natives actually encountered on the river now repeated the Rocky Mountain Indians' warning. They said they never attempted to negotiate these dangerous sections of white water, but always traveled by land when they came to them. Up to now, Alexander had always been a careful man who preferred to lose time rather than take unnecessary chances. But from this period forward, he was audacious, even reckless, in trying to remain on the river, no matter how great the odds against him.

The party met serious trouble on Saturday, May 18, about one hundred miles west of the eastern border of what is now British Columbia. There were animal trails on both sides of the river, leading down to the water from cliffs becoming progressively steeper. These trails appeared every ten yards more or less. But soon the current became much stronger, and so many heavy stones hurtled from the heights into the water that the members of the party were in danger of being hit. Alexander ordered a course steered in mid-stream to avoid the rocks. Because the frozen earth beneath the top layer of soil was melting, the rocks frequently dropped with no advance warning.

A small stone hit one of the hunters on the shoulder but did no damage. Another, larger rock grazed the side of Mackay's head. Had it landed squarely on his skull, it would have killed him. Apprehensions increased. That night, when camp was made on the side of a bluff about five hundred feet above the river, the sound of roaring, churning rapids could be heard in the distance.

Everyone realized that the worst was yet to come, but no one dreamed how frightful the next few days would be. On the morning of Sunday, May 19, the explorers entered Peace River canyon, the first civilized human beings ever to see this mighty phenomenon. The river, which in places had been one mile wide, was hemmed in between cliffs varying in height from six hundred to twelve hundred feet. It was now only one hundred yards wide. Twisting, always churning and boiling, the stream dropped a total of two hundred and seventy feet in a short distance.

The current was so strong that Alexander, Mackay, and the two Indians climbed onto the bank to lighten the load. Finding a beaten path from the river, they followed it and came upon a herd of buffalo. But, before they could kill even one animal, shots came from the river, warning them to return immediately. They hurried back to find the canoe halted by a high waterfall that poured tons of water onto rocks below.

A portage was necessary and precious time was being consumed. The canoe was unloaded, carried ashore, and reloaded, then lifted up the cliffs. The water on the western shore above the waterfall appeared somewhat calmer, so the boat was launched again, with Mackay and the Indians watching from above, prepared to shout a warning if they saw the party headed toward underwater dangers.

For a distance of about one-half mile, the canoe was steered from one side of the river to the other to avoid tremendous rocks. Conditions became too dangerous for anyone to ride, but the precipice was somewhat lower on the east side. So all the men climbed ashore, leaving the cargo in the canoe. The boat was then towed with a strong line three hundred and sixty feet long.

They toiled along the shore until they came to the most rapid cascade yet seen. Alexander took one look at the boiling water and ordered the canoe unloaded and carried past a rocky point. Then it was launched once again, but Alexander feared that it could not remain upright in the water for long.

Mackay was now given charge of the canoe. Alexander, Bishop, and the Indians climbed the cliffs, hoping to direct the efforts of those below. From the heights they could see the dangers ahead. Again and again Alexander shouted at the top of his voice, Bishop and the Indians joining him. But the river, tumbling over rocks, roared so loudly that the men below failed to hear the warnings.

Both groups were in great danger. Those in the canoe were in double jeopardy: at any moment the craft might strike a rock and sink, and stones from the walls of the cliff began once again to drop on the men. Alexander's group on the ledge discovered that the ground beneath their feet was insecure. Repeatedly they took a step forward, only to have the rocks give way. Balancing themselves precariously, testing by advancing one cautious step at a time, they barely avoided being hurled to their deaths in the water below.

After making still another portage, Alexander sent Bishop and one of the Indians ahead to study the water. When they returned, the line was again attached to the canoe. Now everyone except the *voyageurs* walked on the cliff, guiding the boat with the line. Occasionally rocks sawed at the rope and one or another of the men stumbled.

Alexander was consumed by anxiety. He knew that if the men hauling the line made one false step or if the rope itself broke, the canoe and all it contained would be doomed to instant destruction.

The dangers indeed were so great that he decided to scout the waters ahead himself. But once he was out of sight of the canoe and of the men on the cliff, his anxiety increased. It seemed unlikely that anyone would escape without serious injury, and if the canoe were smashed, the expedition would lose all its baggage and be forced to return to civilization.

Each moment Alexander expected someone to come running to him with word that catastrophe had struck. Yet he could not allow himself to dwell on what might happen. He had to make certain the river was navigated; he studied every rock, every whirlpool, every ebb and surge of the current.

After proceeding one hundred to two hundred yards, he would retrace his steps and guide the others forward. This tedious process was repeated countless times.

Late in the afternoon, as Alexander, Mackay, Bishop, and the Indians tugged at the line and while the *voyageurs* in the canoe were poling desperately, the current suddenly threw the prow of the boat against a sharp rock. Water poured in, and the entire cargo seemed about to sink.

The *voyageurs*, however, proved equal to the emergency. They jumped into the river and, with difficulty managing to retain their foothold in chest-high water, carried the canoe to the east bank. The "shore" was only a small ledge, no more than two feet wide, for at that point the cliff was somehow or other almost perpendicular. They hoisted the craft up onto the rocks, then scrambled up onto the little ledge themselves.

Mackay took a single step toward the lip of the cliff. This caused a huge rock to fall into the water below, narrowly missing the *voyageurs*. After that, the men above were forced to use extraordinary care; they moved about as little as possible.

The cargo was unloaded, piece by piece, and the men above used the towing line to haul it up onto the cliff. Then the boat, too, was pulled up. The face of the cliff was too steep for the *voyageurs* to climb; they were hauled up, also, one at a time.

Everyone was exhausted, but Alexander still drove his subordinates firmly. By some miracle most of the cargo was still dry. Two ninety-pound packs of pemmican had been soaked, however; they were opened and left to dry in the sun while the canoe was being repaired.

The hole in the boat was such a long, jagged one that the tired *voyageurs* needed all their skill to repair it. Two ribs had to be replaced, strips of bark had to be sewn over these ribs with *watape*, and the whole prow needed to be gummed.

By the time the cargo had once again been loaded, the soaked pemmican had dried sufficiently to be repacked. Alexander was not satisfied, however; he decided, if possible, to expose it to the sun again the following day.

The repaired canoe was then carried one hundred and fifty paces and launched. The water was a little calmer, so the entire party embarked. After poling a short distance against a viciously strong current, they came to a rocky plateau that stood on the western shore some feet above the water's edge.

There they made camp for the night. But the day's work was not yet finished. The men had to climb the bluff for firewood, the *voyageurs'* clothes had to be dried, and the two packs of pemmican were kept near the fire to rid them of moisture more rapidly.

No more than an hour of daylight remained. Alexander sent Bishop and one of the Indians ahead to see whether conditions on the river ahead had improved. They returned to say that it appeared somewhat calmer, but that rushing water could be heard in the distance. However, Alexander had one consolation that night: the river ran southwest toward the peaks of the Rocky Mountains.

In the morning, the weather was clear, the air sharp. The men started out doggedly, Bishop and the Indians going ahead. The advance group cut through woods, returning after a long absence to report that the river narrowed to a boiling channel no more than fifty yards wide. Alexander went with them now, and saw that the cliffs on both sides were vertical. Since he could not afford to take a chance there, he sent Bishop back with instructions that a portage be made.

Progress continued comparatively good. Alexander kept sending out advance parties. Another portage was made one and one-half miles upstream where the river tumbled over rocks between three-hundred-foot cliffs.

A new problem now presented itself. The river seemed calm enough to be navigated, but the cliffs extended as far ahead as anyone could see and there was no slope that the men could descend to the water. The stone of the cliff, however, was found to be fairly soft; Alexander told the men to use the blunt ends of their axes to chip away steps.

The work was exhausting and slow, but there seemed to be no other solution. Then, when they had only fifteen feet to go before reaching the water, the stone became too hard to chip.

Alexander risked his life now by jumping to a rock that stood up in the river. Reaching it in safety, he beckoned his followers. One by one they climbed down — first onto his shoulders, then onto the rock where he stood.

The canoe was then lowered, inch by inch. But the strain was so great that the boat broke amidships. The men hauled it back up the cliff and repaired it. Then, exercising even greater care, they lowered it once more.

This time they were successful and the voyage was resumed with the aid of poles. When they reached a point beneath an overhanging precipice, the water became so deep that the poles would not touch bottom. The current was even too swift for paddles, so another halt was called. Now Alexander, Mackay, Bishop, and the Indians climbed up the steep slope, attaching the line to the canoe. The *voyageurs* remained in the boat.

The task of towing was not only difficult but dangerous as well. The party on shore had to pass on the outside of trees growing on the very edge of the cliff; the trees were huge poplars, too large in diameter for the line to be passed from hand to hand around them. Repeatedly one or another of the men on the precipice had to seize a precarious toe hold, using iron hooks jabbed into a tree trunk to hold him safe while guiding the canoe below. A single slip would have meant a drop of two hundred to three hundred feet and instant destruction.

The *voyageurs* in the canoe had their own problems, too. The current was so tricky that the boat swung crazily; they had to struggle to prevent it from becoming swamped. The work was fatiguing; three oarsmen rested for a few moments at a time while the other three labored.

When the water became calmer, everybody embarked again, but after they had proceeded a few hundred yards, churning water on the east side made them cross to the west bank. The passage looked so dangerous that the men stripped off their shirts. They reached the west side safely, while Alexander went ahead to measure the height of a range of cliffs.

The exhausted men threw themselves on the ground for a brief rest, but failed to make the line secure. The current promptly seized the canoe and only a lucky accident prevented the craft from being carried away. One of the *voyageurs* still held in his hand the loose end of the rope as he stretched out on the ground. He felt it pulling away, grasped it, and the others hurried to his aid. After a few difficult moments, the canoe was hauled back to safety.

Tracking was resumed; in the next two miles the boat had to be unloaded and reloaded four times. In many places the water was so rough that the experienced *voyageurs* needed all their skill to prevent it from being smashed to pieces on the rocks.

At five o'clock the party was forced to halt. The river had become one gigantic rapid stretching out toward the horizon. After hesitating briefly, Alexander decided to push forward, regardless of the obstacles. After all the baggage was unloaded, it was carried on the backs of the men on shore. The towline was attached to the boat, the *voyageurs* grimly took their seats and tried to run the rapids.

The canoe was hauled only a few feet. A powerful wave snapped the line. It appeared that the craft would founder any moment, for other waves battered her prow. Then a still larger wave threw the craft up onto some rocks on the bank. When the water retreated again, the boat was left high and dry. The *voyageurs* leaped out and pulled the fragile canoe to safety. Miraculously, it had escaped serious damage.

But the men were too shaken to go any farther. The *voyageurs*, after much muttering that the expedition would have to turn back, now declared flatly that there was no alternative. Bishop said little, but he obviously agreed with them. Mackay's silence indicated that he, too, sympathized with their attitude. The Indians, badly frightened, looked as though they might bolt.

But Alexander still would not consider terminating the journey. He ordered the party to climb to the top of a steep, twelve-hundred foot high hill and camp there. In the meantime, he and one of the guides went ahead to see how far the rapids extended.

The hill was almost a sheer cliff, and the men made their way to the top only by cutting down trees which they then used as insecure ladder rungs. Their foothold was precarious, but they managed to gain the crest and build themselves a fire. Then, seeing some elk feeding on the bluffs opposite them, they forgot their tribulations momentarily.

But the river kept reminding them of its awesome power. It roared through a channel no more than fifty yards wide directly below them. Occasionally a huge rock, dislodged from the face of the canyon, would crash below and shatter into countless small stones.

Alexander and the Indian hurried along the ledge as long as daylight remained. They scrambled over boulders, climbed up and down hills, stumbling and falling repeatedly. There seemed to be no end to the rapids, and directly ahead was a five-thousand foot mountain, wooded and with exceptionally steep slopes, that must be crossed. They had reached the Rocky Mountains far sooner than they had expected. But there appeared to be no way to continue the journey.

Returning to the camp site, Alexander admitted that it would be impossible to navigate the rapids. He and his companion were so tired that they were barely able to reach the camp. Their moccasins were worn out, their ankles badly swollen, and they had sustained numerous cuts on the soles and sides of their feet. He stubbornly insisted, however, that a portage could be made, provided that the river again became calm somewhere in the distance.

At three o'clock in the morning, the usual departure hour, a heavy, cold rain began to fall. The men were so disheartened and fatigued, Alexander allowed them to sleep several hours longer. The camp was quiet until eight when the rain ceased.

Now Alexander sent Mackay ahead with Bishop, two of the *voyageurs*, and the Indians. He directed them to scale the mountain and, always keeping the river in sight, to discover whether calm water lay ahead.

XI: THE WILDERNESS ROAD

A GREAT OBSTACLE had been overcome now that the rapids had been passed. Alexander Mackenzie was afraid, however, that no real relief was in sight. Still he kept his foreboding to himself and, while Mackay and his scouts went forward, the rest of the party relaxed for a day.

One of the *voyageurs* discovered wild rice growing in a swamp behind the riverside cliffs and the rest joined him in gathering large quantities of the delicacy. Alexander, meanwhile, went hunting alone. His luck was good; he shot a large elk. After the *voyageurs* had helped him carry it back to the camp, a large fire was lighted. Sugar was boiled with the rice; the men anticipated a feast.

Mackay returned a little before sunset. After leading his group through deep forests, he had climbed high hills and dipped into valleys. It was plain to him that the explorers had now penetrated deep into the Rocky Mountains of what was later to become British Columbia. Yet his report to Alexander was discouraging. To be sure, after climbing to the summit of the nearest mountain, giving him an unimpeded view of the terrain ahead, he had found that the waters of the river were calm but only far in the distance. For the next few miles, however, the Peace was not navigable.

Alexander heard the news in silence, then joined the others at the wilderness banquet. He gave the men double rations of rum, and by the time they finished their meal, their spirits had improved. They promised each other that Mackenzie would think of some way to blaze a trail through the wilderness.

The men went to bed early, but Alexander stayed awake, trying to think of a plan. In order to clear his mind, he set up his astronomical instruments. The clouds remained so thick, however, that he saw nothing in the sky. Nevertheless, he stayed out in the open until long after midnight and, by the time he retired to his tent, he had worked out a scheme of action. His plan promised back-breaking, almost superhuman work for every member of the party, but he thought it should succeed: he intended to cut a road through the wilderness and haul the canoe and supplies right up the mountains!

At daybreak the majority of the men started chopping a road through the forest, up and down hills, to the crest of the mountain directly ahead. They would then make a path down the far side of the steep slope. The trees were small, so Alexander ordered them felled in such a manner that they would lie parallel with the road. But at the same time he ordered that no tree be completely separated from its stump; the trunks were to be left attached to their bases to form a sort of protective railing on either side of the path.

While most of the men were engaged in this task, a small group started to haul the baggage up the steep cliff from the water's edge. The canoe was then pulled up the precipice, a delicate, harrowing task for Alexander and the men helping him.

The boat was reloaded and carried up and down the hills along the road made by the woodsmen. But when they came to the mountain, the incline was too steep for them to carry the canoe. The path was free of underbrush, however, and the men realized the ingenuity of Alexander's scheme.

After the line was doubled, one end was fastened to the boat and the other was looped around a tree stump. Several men pushed and jockeyed the craft, while the man holding the line twisted around the stump pulled with all his strength. Inch by inch, foot by foot, the canoe was dragged higher.

At two o'clock in the afternoon the summit was reached. Even Alexander was impressed by what had been accomplished. The canoe, laden with three thousand pounds of baggage, had been literally hauled up the side of a mountain.

Everyone was so tired that a meal was eaten, then the men sprawled on the ground to rest. At five o'clock Alexander ordered the road-cutting resumed, and the men felled trees for about a mile. Then, stumbling back to the camp, they ate quickly, going off to sleep almost immediately.

But the leader again set up his telescope. At ten o'clock he observed an emersion of Jupiter's second satellite.

This success raised his spirits and, even though the hour was late, he went to see the river. The Peace here had contracted to a width of thirty-five yards, flowing with tremendous force between bluffs of sheer rock six hundred feet high on either side of the channel. The water made no sound, although it rushed with astonishing speed. As he watched with the aid of a bright moon, the water rose higher in the channel. From marks on both sides of the cliffs, he judged that in coming days the Peace would reach a point near the tops of the bluffs.

On Thursday, May 23, the weather cleared. Some men carried the canoe and baggage, while others engaged in the wearisome task of cutting the road. To speed the operation, Alexander joined this group and wielded an axe with ferocious energy.

In the afternoon the ground became very uneven as the woodsmen made their way up steep hills, then down deep defiles. They had come now to a portion of the countryside where a forest fire had raged some years earlier. Trunks of trees laid low by the fire were spread out everywhere. The underbrush was heavy; the men had to squirm through large patches of briars that cut their skin and clothing.

Nevertheless they made better progress than Alexander had anticipated. The carriers did not catch up with the cutters until four o'clock in the afternoon. Because the men had been toiling steadily for twelve hours, Alexander called a halt for the day. He estimated that they had traveled only three miles since their early-morning start.

Two elk and a caribou were shot in the forest. While dinner was being prepared, Alexander went off again to study the river. The prospect was not encouraging. The stream no longer followed a twisting course, to be sure, but as far ahead as the leader could see, it flowed in an almost straight passage, tossing in high, foaming, half-formed billows.

He was discouraged, realizing that at least another day or two of grinding labor awaited the men before they reached the upper end of the canyon. Nevertheless, he felt sure there was an end in view. Having already overcome so many seemingly impassable obstacles, he was determined to push on with all possible speed.

When he returned to the camp, his personnel was clustered around a natural spring that bubbled up from a bed of ice and snow. Tired and out of sorts, he was about to rebuke the men for wasting time, but paused when he saw expressions of wonder on their faces. He joined them, and at Mackay's urging, tested the water emerging from the spring. To his amazement, it was hot.

His scientific curiosity was aroused. At first he assumed that beds of coal were burning beneath the surface of the ground, and, in spite of his fatigue, he began to dig, aided by Mackay. But they found no coal beds; the rocky soil beneath the top layer of earth was cold. Since no one could explain the mystery, the Indian guides grew uneasy.

But the other members of the party, emotionally and physically exhausted, wanted to relax. Bishop found some duck eggs in *a* nest, placed one in the spring, and, after a few minutes, cracked it. Everyone shouted triumphantly when it was seen that the egg had been boiled hard. After that, the *voyageurs* could not resist the temptation to hard-boil the rest of the eggs. Then Mackay cut up some parsnips, cooking them in a small pot over the water. By this time, Alexander himself was so intrigued that he tried his hand at the game. The men cheered him vigorously when he succeeded in boiling coffee over the spring.

The guides soon lost their fear of the mysterious hot water; they were proud of themselves when they, too, boiled a few chunks of elk meat. All the men were behaving like children now, laughing wildly each time a new dish was cooked.

Alexander then filled a metal cup with water from the spring. After it had cooled, he sipped it. It was potable, although the taste seemed faintly bitter. Believing that the holiday mood would help the men to take their minds off their worries, he issued rum all around and himself filled their cups with boiling spring water. The experiment was an unqualified success.

A moment later Bishop announced that he wanted a soft-boiled egg; the men scattered to hunt for another duck's nest. When one was found, several eggs were soft-boiled. Each member of the party tested them; everyone agreed that no more delicious dish had ever been prepared. But Mackay said that he liked his eggs salted, so still another search was made. No more eggs were found, however, and the merriment gradually subsided.

While the festivities were in progress, another enigma, this one man-made, caught Alexander's attention. Near the camp were many stumps. The trees had been felled to make a meandering path rather like the one the explorers had been cutting. This road more or less followed the course of the river, but wandered frequently some distance from the canyon. Whoever had made the path had followed a line of least resistance, avoiding the heights when possible.

A close study of the fallen trees and stumps showed Alexander's experienced woodsmen that the path had been made the previous year. And what was more, the task had been performed with axes of metal rather than of the stone the Indian tribes of the area used. To the best of Alexander's knowledge, no other party of explorers from the civilized world had been in the area. Certainly none had penetrated this far west. He speculated that the cutting had been done by Cree Indians, equipped with the tools of civilization. Yet it was difficult to believe that the Cree, with game and furs so plentiful in their own domain, would wander that far from home.

The following morning, while his subordinates patched the canoe with gum and made themselves new poles, Alexander decided to leave a message for any natives who might pass that way. First he cut and trimmed a tall, straight, poplar sapling; this he stuck firmly in the ground. Now he tied on it a knife, a fire-making flint-and-steel, several strings of beads, and a small looking glass of highly burnished metal.

One of the guides, Cancre the Crab, followed his example, leaving a message of his own. He chewed one end of a green stick until it resembled a brush, then tied the end to the marker. All northwest Indians used such sticks to pick marrow out of bones; so his token meant that the region abounded in game.

The difficult journey was resumed shortly before daybreak. The men continued to cut a road up and down slopes of exceptionally steep hills; they were slowed when they were forced to slash a road through a forest of towering pines. Alexander almost wished he was following the path previously used by the unknown Indians. But even with the extra labor involved, his own method was faster. And as travel had been so slow in recent days, speed once again had become a primary consideration. No one knew what obstacles lay ahead or how long they might need to reach the Pacific. The Scotsman still wanted to complete his round-trip journey before the coming of winter, and even though it was still May, the hazardous toil of travel would devour weeks and months.

At four o'clock in the afternoon the party reached the upper end of the canyon. Beyond it the river was smooth and broad although fast-flowing. Alexander estimated that melting snow in the mountains was causing the waters to rise at a rate of from one to two feet a day.

Nevertheless, the rapids were behind now. The weary travelers, their canoe and cumbersome baggage intact, continued for another one hundred yards, and then made camp on a level stretch of ground. That night the sound of the hissing, bubbling rapids could be heard but faintly, and the men slept well.

On the twenty-five mile climb through the canyon, the explorers had been moving steadily into higher ground. They now stood on a plateau. Directly ahead were mammoth, snow-covered peaks. They had finally reached the heart of the Rocky Mountains.

Soon, if all went well, Alexander would test the theory first advocated by Peter Pond. He would discover whether the rivers on the far side of the mountains flowed toward the west. Logic told him they did. But, as he had learned already to his sorrow, logic was not necessarily a safe rule to follow when exploring uncharted territory.

Although anxious to discover the truth as soon as possible, he had to curb his eagerness. He himself could double his pace without faltering, but the other members of the party could not. Even Mackay and Bishop, far stronger than ordinary outdoorsmen, were exhausted now. The Indian guides were so tired they swallowed their pride and begged for a few extra hours of sleep. Even the extraordinary *voyageurs* complained of muscle aches and of legs that were more than a trifle shaky. So the party remained in camp on Saturday, May 25, to recuperate.

The explorers had now reached ground where the weather, particularly at night, was bitter cold. The men tried sleeping the way they did in chilly weather, leaving one side of their tents open and facing a large fire. But when they did not warm themselves sufficiently, they imitated the Indians of the Arctic by rolling themselves in their blankets just a short distance from the flames. The weather, Alexander feared, was only a foretaste of worse to come.

What bothered him even more was the knowledge that the party had traveled a meager two hundred and fifty miles in thirteen days. The rugged mountains ahead looked ominous; nobody knew how many other chains, still higher and more difficult to traverse, lay beyond the first range.

To add to the complications, in the distance Alexander could see a ridge that marked a line of demarcation of two rivers emptying into the Peace. One flowed in from the north, the other from the south. Which should he follow?

An elderly Indian, who had visited his winter camp on the Peace River, was supposed to have spent much time in the area during his youth as a member of various war parties. This elder had warned Mackenzie under no circumstances to take the northern fork. The southern one would lead the band of explorers to the highest crests of the peaks, the Indian had said, and beyond that river were connecting waterways that would carry them to their desired goal. But if they went north, they would lose themselves in a glacial wilderness.

Alexander could not know, of course, if the Indian's advice had been accurate. The Peace River actually splits into two branches just east of the Continental Divide. The branch flowing from the north, now called the Finlay, runs through a narrow valley and dries to a mere trickle high in the mountains of the north. The southern branch, now called the Parsnip River, provides a difficult but nevertheless attainable passage to the Pacific. A series of glacier-fed lakes located near the Continental Divide permits portages to a small stream, now known as the Bad River, which flows west and then conveniently twists through the mountains toward the south.

A major branch called the Blackwater emerges from it, but the Blackwater is choked off by the coastal range of mountains. The Bad, if followed on its main course, leads to another and stronger river, the Fraser. The latter runs south, then turns to the west and empties into salt water between the mainland of British Columbia and Vancouver Island.

Mackenzie did not know about the existence of the Fraser. His concern was with the Finlay, and his major problem was whether to follow the Finlay to the north or the Parsnip to the south.

His dilemma was compounded by the fact that the northern branch seemed far more tranquil. The *voyageurs* would be able to paddle up it, even though they would be moving against the current. The turbulent southern fork was wilder. The men were not pleased by the prospect of poling the canoe for weary days on end, and they urged the leader to take the northern branch. Alexander promised to sleep on the matter.

When he awoke on the morning of Sunday, May 26, he had made up his mind. A man devoted to science but who now lacked all scientific knowledge to guide him, he had concluded that he must rely on the old Indian who had urged him to choose the Parsnip. So, for better or worse, he would follow the southern branch of the Peace that twisted and turned as it fell from the great peaks of the Rocky Mountains.

XII: ACROSS THE GREAT DIVIDE

THE MEN WERE DEPRESSED and grumbled because Alexander had not taken the north fork. He tried to tell them he himself would have been inclined to travel on that river, but that he felt it wise to follow the advice of the old Indian. Neither the *voyageurs* nor the guides, their nerves raw after passing through the canyon, accepted his explanation, so he dropped the subject.

The men alternately poled and tracked all that day. This was actually fatiguing labor. But after the ordeal they had experienced, it seemed comparatively easy. The party covered thirty miles. The river bottom was favorable for poling. The portages, to be sure, were fairly long but were made over slowly rising ground littered with few obstacles.

The party had difficulty finding a camping site that night, a problem that would plague them for many nights to come. The fast-rising waters, swelling to floodtide proportions in the spring thaw, spread out over a considerable area. There were few hills on the rocky plateau to protect the company during a halt for sleep.

At two o'clock in the morning, the men awoke when the waters extinguished their fire, soaked their blankets, and seeped into part of their baggage. Thereafter they tried to exercise still greater care in selecting a bivouac area, but similar accidents continued to annoy them and disturb their rest.

Alexander, as always, was spending his own energies with reckless abandon, so occasionally he took short naps in the canoe to compensate for sleepless nights. At one point, while he was dozing, he lost a notebook containing all his entries of the previous week. Horrified by the loss, he assumed that the book had been brushed overboard by an overhanging tree branch.

That night, relying completely on memory, he painstakingly reconstructed the information he had written. In all, he spent three long nights at the task.

One afternoon the explorers approached some dangerous cascades, forcing them to carry the canoe and its cargo overland for several hundred yards. Alexander was particularly careful to mark the spot on his map and to study the area directly above the rapids. From above the rapids, the appearance of the water gave no hint that rapids were nearby, nor could the men hear any increase in the roar of the river. Still, the hidden danger of rapids served as a constant reminder to the men that death always hovered near, ready to snatch them.

A heavy rain mixed with sleet forced the company to remain in camp until noon the following day. During this period of enforced leisure, the nets were set. Large numbers of the rainbow-flecked trout were caught — beautiful fish, measuring from ten to fourteen inches, their dorsal fins as high as their bodies were deep. Alexander suspected that some of the small streams flowing toward the north were the headwaters of the great river that now bore his name. He called these fish "Arctic trout," having seen some like them on his previous journey.

Trout actually were the last food, other than wild parsnips, that the party found for some time. The next week they subsisted exclusively on pemmican, sometimes boiled with parsnips tops.

In the nightmare that followed, the men had difficulty keeping count of the days and remembering the date. They were now making their way up through the highest portion of the Rockies, encased in a world of frozen horror. The river was too narrow and turbulent for the canoe to be floated, but they had no guide other than the stream. So they climbed and scrambled up into the heights along its rock-strewn, slippery bank.

Wild life became increasingly scarce. Mackay saw a single moose in the distance, but it vanished before he could raise his rifle to his shoulder. A guide caught a glimpse of a solitary beaver; it, too, disappeared. Both natives became completely terror-stricken; they said the party was entering a world cursed by their gods.

The *voyageurs* suspected that the Indians might be right; Bishop himself was inclined to agree. Mackay kept a tight grip on his emotions, afraid of losing his sanity if he gave full expression to his feelings. Only Alexander remained outwardly unperturbed; even his notes did not reflect the hell the party was forced to endure. He thought it unmanly to dwell on the terrors of the mountain heights. Besides, he did not want to be accused at some later date of exaggeration. However, Mackay, knowing that his superior was keeping a most laconic record, wrote fuller accounts in his own diary.

The men struggled above the timber line; there was no wood now for fires. The oxygen in the air diminished. The explorers' legs felt as heavy as lead; they found it a torture to carry the boat and its cargo.

When the sun came out, it burned the toughened skin of the men. The glare on the snow made their eyes water and sometimes blinded them.

Occasionally they dipped into little wooded valleys, where again and again they had to cut trails, making railings of felled trees as they had done in the Peace River canyon.

But even when they found wood, it was always difficult — and sometimes impossible — to light substantial fires. Usually the flames flickered for a short time, then expired. Water, ice, and snow were plentiful, yet it became impossible to boil even a small amount of liquid.

The men were so cold that Alexander gave them rum, but one or two swallows made even the robust *voyageurs* ill.

Venomous rattlesnakes, which the Indians believed to be the reincarnated spirits of their enemies, glided into the open from behind high rocks. Even Alexander lost count of how many snakes were shot.

The hungry *voyageurs*, heartily sick of cold, greasy pemmican, wanted to cook some of the dead rattlesnakes. But when they could not make a fire large enough, they considered eating the snakes raw. The guides threatened to bolt.

The whole world became an endless mass of bare limestone, craggy and windswept.

Then the river was reduced to a mere trickle between two mammoth peaks. The panicky men feared it would disappear altogether, leaving them stranded. Alexander insisted that his instruments gave him accurate observations of their location, but the men did not believe him. So frightened they scarcely knew what they were doing, they kept coming to him, begging him to demonstrate that the marvelous tools of science were really effective. He told them to be patient.

The heavily laden canoe was dragged by two men now, land-pushed by two others. The work was so exhausting that the teams of porters had to change every half-hour.

Alexander, driving the party mercilessly, urged the men onward. Soon, he promised, they would reach the last heights and the journey would become easier. Instead, they saw another, somewhat higher, range of peaks directly ahead.

This was the most crushing blow so far. The *voyageurs* wanted to turn back. Alexander declared that he would force no one to accompany him, but insisted he would press on alone if necessary.

But the party was so dependent on his leadership that they staggered up the last steep slopes. Sometimes they were so tired that they crawled on their hands and knees. Half-crazed, they wanted to abandon the canoe and supplies. Mackay and Bishop collected all the firearms; then Alexander, drawing his pistols and cocking them, insisted that the boat and cargo must not be left behind. The men continued to haul and shove sullenly. Alexander set an example; he spent hours tugging at the towline. The rope sawed into his shoulder until it bit into raw flesh, yet he would not give up.

The river, continuing to flow down toward the east from the heights above, still beckoned, taunting them.

Worn-out boots had to be cut off feet and ankles swollen to double normal size. The men then wrapped their feet in cloths which were soon reduced to rags.

The current of the river slackened, the water became shallower. Alexander was afraid the prophecy of the old Indian would prove meaningless and that he and his men would be stranded in a mountain wilderness. Then, unexpectedly, the current again gathered force as it passed through a narrow, miles-long gorge. Almost inexplicably, the water became calm, so the canoe was patched and launched.

Poling was resumed now. The river dipped below timber-line, and deep forests were seen on both sides of the fantastically beautiful gorge. Beaver seemed to be everywhere. The Indians shot a moose, then a caribou. Mackay went ashore, too, to lighten the load, and flushed out and shot several plump, large geese. At last the company would have fresh meat to eat again.

The canoe emerged from the gorge at last. The *voyageurs* found a high, dry spot to camp for the night. Mackay and the natives found they had to build a raft to carry their kill, then swim across the river to the bivouac — the oarsmen by accident had camped on an island.

No one minded the inconvenience, however. Plenty of wood was available, and the party looked forward to a feast. The starved men were almost delirious at the very thought of food. They drank their daily ration of rum while gathering kindling; the atmosphere became festive.

But Alexander Mackenzie remained remote, lost in deep contemplation. He had watched the course carefully as the voyage had been made through the gorge, past innumerable beaver dams and through small lakes into which the roots of great poplars and pines jutted. He was confused, utterly bewildered and heartsick. For the current still flowed toward the east.

One day the river rose by two feet, swollen by melted snow that the rains had sent cascading down the mountains. Progress was slowed to a crawl. The current was too swift for the men to paddle the canoe upstream, too deep for them to use their poles. Trees, many of them willows, were so thick along the banks that only one brief attempt was made to use the towline.

The men were forced to haul themselves upstream from branch to branch. That day they traveled only two miles. The next they made four, then three on the day after that.

Alexander wrote in his notebook that he was lost, but he did not confide in anyone — even Mackay. All of his calculations appeared wrong. After struggling across the high mountains, the experiences the party was undergoing now were distinctly anticlimactic. According to the theory on which the entire future of the expedition depended, the rivers west of the great Rocky Mountain spine or backbone of the North American continent should flow toward the Pacific. Yet they kept running eastward.

Mackenzie pinned his flagging hopes on the fact that they were still traveling through a long, wooded pass in the mountains. Perhaps they had not yet actually reached the Continental Divide. Nature, as he had discovered repeatedly, was deceptive.

He pondered constantly on the problem, and even wondered whether the Continental Divide itself actually existed. It might be only a figment of imagination. He tried to comfort himself by re-reading Captain Cook's account of his discoveries. Cook specifically stated that there were rivers emptying into the Pacific. Therefore, bodies of water — somewhere — must flow west.

On June 9, at a point somewhere on the southern reaches of the Parsnip, the expedition's luck changed with breathtaking suddenness. In mid-afternoon, the smell of a cooking fire was strong in the air. Since human beings must be in the vicinity, Alexander ordered his men to lower their voices and proceed with great care. Within a few minutes the party heard tree branches and twigs breaking in the underbrush near the north bank of the river. A man called out something in a deep voice and was answered by a terrified woman.

Alexander wanted desperately to obtain information from the natives, but he feared they might become frightened and disappear in the forest. In order to reassure them he ordered the *voyageurs* to head for the south bank of the river.

The Scottish leader was taking a great risk, for his party's rifles were not even primed. If attacked, his men could not respond immediately. They would become the easy prey of a large war party. He had no idea how many Indians might be in the forest.

When the canoe reached mid-stream, two warriors clad in loin cloths and skin capes appeared on a high rock at the water's edge. Brandishing crude spears and threatening the travelers with bows and arrows, they began to shout. Although they spoke in a strange tongue, their meaning was clear. They were ordering the intruders to leave.

When Alexander's canoe finally reached the south bank, he told his subordinates to sit still and say nothing. Eventually the Indians' fears subsided. When the explorers went ashore, the natives clustered around Alexander. In all, the Indian party consisted of three families.

Alexander ordered his canoe hauled up, the baggage unloaded, and the tents pitched. While his men were thus occupied, Alexander and Cancre, his interpreter, parlayed with the natives. The Scotsman smiled until his face ached; Cancre kept assuring the natives that he meant them no harm. When one of the ninety-pound packages had been brought to Alexander, he opened it with the air of a conjurer, giving each Indian a string of beads. The squaws received mirrors; the men and older boys, steel knives.

They compared these gifts with knives of their own. Their own weapons were made of iron, almost positive proof that they were in contact with Pacific coast traders. Alexander refrained from questioning them, however, until all the amenities had been observed.

Pemmican and parched corn were served, the two parties eating together. At last the natives seemed to feel at ease, so

Alexander asked his first question: Where had they acquired their iron weapons?

Their reply was long and rambling. They told him how beaver and moose skins were prepared deep in the interior of the wilderness, then sent by means of a succession of tribes to a great sea called "The Stinking Lake." On that lake, they said, the local Indians traded with strangers who came to them in ships as large as huge islands.

Alexander knew now beyond all doubt that the Pacific lay ahead.

Then he remembered that the old Indian at the Peace River headquarters had told him it would be about a day's portage after he came to the headwaters of the Parsnip River. Where, he asked now, was the great body of water that moved toward the southwest and eventually fed into the sea?

The natives did not give him a direct answer. In one more day — perhaps a little less, they hinted, the strangers would reach the end of the Parsnip.

Alexander tried repeatedly to glean more information, but failed. Finally he realized that the natives were lying at the request of Cancre who wanted to go home.

When he confronted the Indians with his suspicions, the truth came out at last. They admitted knowledge of a great river running toward the southwest and emptying into The Stinking Lake. One of its bigger branches was only a short distance away, a single day's portage from the headwaters of the Parsnip.

The news was almost too good to be true. Alexander leaped into the air jubilantly.

Then he asked that a member of the party accompany him, promising in return a pistol, ammunition and gunpowder. One of the warriors volunteered to take the position; he was immediately accepted. Alexander was so anxious to get started that his party broke camp at once, even though some of the men had not even finished their breakfast. As they parted with the other members of the band, Alexander urged them to meet him at the same spot in precisely "two moons' time."

The advice of the old Indian at the Peace River headquarters had proved to be accurate. Mackenzie was his old self again, confident and full of unquenchable vitality.

The new guide drew a crude map on a piece of birchbark with a stub of charcoal. Alexander kept this chart close beside him for the next day and a half as the expedition advanced rapidly. The current gradually became weaker, the channel narrower, and paddles could be used once again. As the canoe shot upstream, everyone realized that they were nearing the headwaters. Excitement kept mounting all day.

The following morning, oblivious to the cold, the explorers got an early start. They continued to paddle upstream until noon. Then their new guide directed them to follow a small branch of the Parsnip scarcely ten yards wide. It twisted incessantly, often doubling back on itself.

Now Alexander found that, both ahead and behind, the earth seemed to drop away. There were, to be sure, mountains to the south and north, but none appeared higher than the ground over which they were now traveling. Common sense told him that if the Continental Divide really existed, the expedition was fast approaching it.

The *voyageurs* continued to paddle steadily. Within an hour, they reached a mountain lake swollen by melted snow. When Alexander beheld a magnificent view off toward the northeast, he realized that this lake was one of the headwaters of the Mackenzie River. After four years of labor and planning, he had found the source of the great river bearing his name.

When the party reached the far side of the lake, Alexander gestured sharply. The canoe glided to a halt. Unable to speak, he pointed toward several small streams.

They were flowing westward!

That moment was the most gratifying Alexander Mackenzie had ever known. At two o'clock in the afternoon of June 12, 1793, he proved that Peter Pond's theory about the great rivers of North America was correct. And, at the same time, he verified the existence of a Continental Divide.

The canoe did not halt for more than a minute or two. But no one spoke or stirred until Alexander raised his hand again. Then the *voyageurs* resumed paddling, the guide directing them toward a river that opened out of the western side of the lake.

The boat moved into it, the men were jubilant. For weary weeks they had been struggling upstream; now they were going downstream. *They were actually moving with the tide — not against it!*

XIII: CATASTROPHE ON THE BAD RIVER

THE VOYAGE DOWNSTREAM continued for only a short distance. Then the explorers came to the portage mentioned by the old Indian at the Peace River camp. A low ridge of land stood directly ahead. On the banks of the little river were strewn canoes, stone axes, and other weapons left there by Indians who, apparently, intended to retrieve them at some later date.

The guide led the company through an overland ravine of eight hundred and seventeen paces. The men carried the canoe and cargo, then launched the boat again when they came to another lake. No one seemed to notice the bitter cold. Bishop even laughed heartily when he fell into a snowbank. The men believed they had conquered the wilderness and that the Pacific must be directly ahead.

The canoe was paddled across this second lake, then through a small channel connecting with a third lake. Emerging from this body of water, the party found themselves in a stream so small it scarcely could be called a river. It contained a great deal of driftwood; the passage became so difficult that Mackay, Bishop, and the three guides walked along on shore to lighten the load.

Soon the channel grew broader, the water ran more swiftly. But the river still contained so much driftwood that the party had to cut a channel through it. Beds of gravel, enlarged by rushes of water in the spring thaws, and uprooted trees further impeded progress. The men had to jump into the water again and again to prevent the canoe from grounding. Each time they went overboard, the shock of the chilly water numbed them. The river was fed by melting snow and was as cold as ice. Some spots were so tangled that short portages had to be made.

Meanwhile, the land party, too, was encountering great difficulties. Brambles in the woods grew seven to eight feet high, so a path had to be hacked out of the wilderness.

The current became increasingly swift; Alexander grew apprehensive. Fearing rapids ahead, he sent Mackay and two of the Indians to investigate even though the canoe-men had to wait while they cut themselves a path.

Soon the three returned to report rapids and whirlpools, uprooted trees and huge boulders in the river. The voyage continued. Another portage was necessary when the rapids were encountered, and the men were exhausted. But since it was not yet night, Alexander was eager to press forward.

He suggested that he himself should join the shore party to lighten still more the load in the canoe. But the *voyageurs* earnestly begged him to remain; if they perished, they wanted him to die with them.

The river, soon to be called the Bad, lived up to its future name. The men were experiencing the greatest difficulty trying to control the boat. Never east of the Rocky Mountains had they encountered such dangerous water; they were badly frightened. A short distance on, the boat swept downstream sideways; the *voyageurs* fought the current in a vain attempt to regain command of the craft. Suddenly the canoe struck an underwater rock or sandbar, smashing its stern.

Alexander instantly jumped into the water, trying to halt the boat. The men followed his example, gripping the sides. The current, however, was so strong that it swept them downstream, still holding onto the boat. The water became deeper now; it soon was over their heads. They were unable to save themselves or their cargo. Then the boat struck another rock which caved in the bow. Before the men could halt the runaway, the river carried them — and the canoe, too — over rapids that ripped holes in the bottom of the boat.

One of the men reached out to grasp the branch of a tree, caught it, and was thrown almost to the far bank. He managed to scramble ashore with the help of the horrified shore party. Nothing, however, could be done to save those in the water.

The river continued to carry canoe and men downstream, careening them madly from one side of the water to the other. Miraculously, the frame held together, even though the interior of the boat was flooded. Alexander and the *voyageurs* clung to the wreck with all their remaining strength, knowing that if they loosened their holds they would be tom apart by the jagged rocks.

They continued downstream on their nightmare voyage, completely helpless. Gradually the wrecked boat flattened out as it filled more and more. The cargo was so heavy that it continued to give the battered men some measure of support; what was left of the boat could not be overturned.

Then, after several hundred yards, they came at last to shallow water. Utterly exhausted and so numbed by the cold that they could barely move. Alexander and the *voyageurs* dragged themselves, their precious cargo, and the hulk of the canoe out onto the shore. The land party came up to help them, but when the Indians saw the wreckage, they burst into tears. Instead of helping, they just sat down on the ground, weeping and lamenting.

Alexander had no time to coddle them. Afraid that part of the cargo had fallen to the bottom of the river through the many holes in the canoe, he plunged back into the chest-high water. As he had suspected, several ninety-pound packages were resting on the gravel bed. The men rushed to help him. Eventually all the provisions were hauled ashore.

No one now was allowed to fling himself on the ground to rest. Alexander wanted to learn what supplies had been lost and, of those portions still safe, how much had been ruined by the water. Apparently most of the ammunition was missing. The weight of the lead balls had carried the packages containing them to the bottom. Several kettles and other iron objects had been lost, and two ninety-pound packages of pemmican had been so soaked through that they were useless.

By some miracle, however, the gunpowder was dry; it had been wrapped in several layers of heavily oiled cloth. Alexander's scientific instruments were intact, as were his books. And the greater part of the emergency food supplies would be edible after drying out.

The loss of the bullets was not irreparable, fortunately. Alexander had planned the expedition so carefully that he had packed a number of bars of lead and several bullet presses. The men would be able to make new ammunition.

A huge fire was lighted; all the supplies of fresh meat were cooked and everyone was given a double portion of rum. With the company in a semi-hysterical state, Alexander realized he faced one of the gravest crises of the trip. At the moment his followers were grateful to be alive, but when they became calmer, he knew that they would urge him to turn back. Anticipating their demand, he acted now with great care.

He said nothing until the fire, food and rum had restored their energy. Then he made a speech. Saying that he knew precisely how they felt he reminded them that they were still alive and well. They had suffered a bad fright, but before starting out on the journey he had told them that they would be exposed to dangers. Surely they were not such weaklings that they would even contemplate giving up their search for the Pacific now. Surely they were not such cowards that they would shrink from fresh dangers. He teased them so gently, they grew ashamed of their fears. Then he heaped praise on them, reminding them they were men of the north, whose courage and resolution had justly won the admiration of the entire world.

His talk had the desired effect, at least for the moment. The men agreed to follow wherever he might lead them.

After that, he put them to work at once. By the light of the fire, they patched the canoe with bark, oil-cloth, and large quantities of gum. Only when the craft was seaworthy did Alexander call a halt to the day's activities.

He allowed the men to sleep a little later the next morning. Then they went to work obtaining new bark and gum, fashioning struts for the canoe to replace those broken, and carefully drying the cargo before the fire. While they labored, he went into the forest and shot a moose so they could eat heartily again that evening.

The next day's work was exhausting. The men made countless portages past rapids and whirlpools, uprooted trees and huge boulders that jutted menacingly out of the water. They had to cut their way through tangled jams of driftwood. Moreover, the canoe needed still more strengthening.

They did not halt until seven o'clock that night. Everyone except Alexander was discouraged. In fourteen hours they had only traveled three miles.

One of the *voyageurs* rebelled, saying he would go no farther. Alexander chose ridicule to whip the malcontent into line. The man was the most simple-minded of the *voyageurs*. Alexander teased him until all the others were roaring with laughter, and the rebel grinned sheepishly. The mutiny was ended.

The next day's journey was even worse. Early in the morning the party came to a high waterfall; a road had to be cut through a muddy swamp to make a portage. The mud was ankle-deep; many roots hidden underfoot caused the men to trip and sprawl on their faces in the bog. Clouds of mosquitoes and sand flies appeared to plague them. The canoe had become so heavy after repeated gumming applications that two men could carry it and its cargo only one hundred yards before another two must take their places. Again they lost count of the number of portages they made. At dusk, when a halt was called, Alexander estimated that once more they had covered only two miles.

That night the native guide who had joined them near the Continental Divide vanished.

For six exhausting days the men plodded through the swampy morass, often fighting through thigh-deep slime, constantly tormented by mosquitoes. Mackay and Cancre, who had gone off in search of the missing guide, returned to report no sign of him. The *voyageurs* became so discouraged that they talked to each other constantly about turning back. Alexander pretended not to hear them; he tried to hearten them with stories of the easy sailing they would enjoy when they came to the great river ahead.

On June 18 they at last reached a large body of water, two hundred yards wide, smooth and clear, flowing swiftly to the west. Alexander let the men assume that this was the river he had been seeking; he himself suspected it was only a branch. Still, the canoe was launched and the troubles of the preceding days were almost forgotten as the craft shot smoothly downstream for mile after peaceful mile.

The river opened into a lake where the current was weaker, then the explorers came to a river a half-mile wide. Alexander now felt positive they had reached the stream for which he had been searching. In the distance, deep in the forests that lined both banks, they saw fires showing Indians must be nearby. But they caught no glimpse of any natives.

On June 19 their progress was even faster; the canoe glided rapidly down the river that, in time to come would be known as the Fraser.

Late in the morning they came to a canyon. On both sides were high, white cliffs, their tops crowned with pinnacles formed in odd and grotesque shapes. Gradually the river grew narrower, becoming only about fifty yards wide. The men suspected that rapids must be ahead, a guess that proved to be right. They went ashore to carry the canoe and cargo and happily discovered traces of an Indian trail obviously already used as a portage.

Joy changed to dismay when they found the path had to be widened for their cumbersome canoe. An hour later they came to another, smaller canyon and again went ashore when they heard the sound of a waterfall ahead. A second portage was made, but the boat was so heavy that it cracked and broke while two *voyageurs* were carrying it on their shoulders.

The cargo had to be unloaded now so the canoe might be repaired — an irritating, fatiguing task taking the better part of four hours. Everyone realized that another boat must be made. The old, battered craft was now so heavy that two men found it difficult to carry, even when empty. No birch trees were visible in the nearby forests, however, so their patched boat had to serve for the time being, regardless of the inconvenience. Hating the canoe now as intensely as if it were a living creature, the exhausted men resumed the voyage.

On Tuesday, June 20, the countryside gradually changed. The high banks of the river fell away, and the stream itself sped through a broad, thickly wooded valley. On both banks, small hills were visible at the horizon. The forest consisted of towering cypress and poplar trees. Later in the day the party came upon cottonwood, willow, and birch. There was virtually no underbrush.

Then, amazingly, close to the bank they saw a huge house, and Alexander called a halt. It was the first carpentered "long" house he had found west of Michilimackinac, and he examined it in detail. It was thirty feet long and twenty feet wide, with three low-set doors and three large fireplaces. Beds were built along the walls. Apparently the place had been made to house three Indian families.

Constructed of straight, tough spruce timbers, its roof was supported by a ridgepole resting on two ten-foot-high forked poles of cedar. The logs were lashed together with branches of cedar, and the structure was virtually water-and air-tight. Directly under the roof were poles for hanging and drying fish.

Most of the space inside the dwelling was occupied by an ingenious, intricate, man-made device so large that it could have been removed only by tearing down an entire wall of the house. Resembling an elongated egg in shape, it consisted of long pieces of split wood with rounded ends, each as thick as a finger and placed approximately one inch apart. After studying the contraption, Alexander and Mackay concluded that it must be a fish snare. They also surmised that the house was used as a summer residence. Its inhabitants would appear soon, for the weather was growing warmer each day.

The explorers could not wait to greet these natives, however. Alexander still felt a sense of urgency. His first step was to get a new canoe made as soon as possible. A short distance beyond the native dwelling the party passed a river flowing into the Fraser through thickly wooded land. Birch trees were appearing with greater frequency now, and they were becoming taller. Several stops were made to cut bark. In all, enough was collected for a new canoe thirty feet long and four and one-half feet deep. But cedar, hickory, and other kinds of wood needed for the framework were still lacking. The old boat, therefore, could not yet be abandoned.

By now, it had become so heavy and cumbersome that the *voyageurs* actually preferred to shoot a dangerous rapid rather than carry the canoe across a half-mile portage. The boat somehow survived this new battering, but it had to be gummed and patched again before the men could proceed.

Game was becoming increasingly scarce at this juncture. But Alexander, thinking of the future, decided to store away two ninety-pound packages of pemmican. A hole was dug, then filled in again. The cache was planted deep enough so that a fire could have been built directly over the food without damaging it. Notches were placed on the trunks of several nearby trees to identify the site. From that time on, Alexander buried a number of such packages of pemmican.

A few miles farther downstream a party of Indians was encountered. The members of the expedition saw a small canoe pulled up on the bank of the river. A moment later, a native in another canoe came in sight. The brave was astonished by the appearance of the heavily gummed boat and its crew. Leaping ashore, he shouted at the top of his voice.

Several other warriors appeared from the woods, all armed with bows and arrows. Determined to take no chances, they warned the strangers not to approach, and accompanied their words and gestures with showers of arrows. One brave, jumping into a canoe, paddled furiously downstream, obviously intending to alert his people to the enemies at hand.

Directing his subordinates to paddle to the far bank, Alexander disembarked there. Both his guides kept repeating that he meant the natives no harm, but the warriors were too excited to hear a word. Something dramatic and simple must be done at once to save the situation.

XIV: DIPLOMAT IN BUCKSKINS

NEVER HAD Alexander Mackenzie displayed greater courage than he showed now on the banks of the Fraser River as he and his party faced the band of excited, angry Indian warriors. And rarely had his quick mind functioned as rapidly and incisively.

He needed guides if he hoped to reach his goal, the shores of the Pacific Ocean. He realized, too, that he could not frighten the local natives into submission. The region through which he was traveling was too heavily populated. Rifles might cow one band of braves — or a dozen — but his company was too small to survive if the Indians decided to wage wholesale war.

So he must win their help and friendship. Perhaps from his childhood in the Hebrides, he remembered the old proverb: sugar catches more flies than vinegar.

Whatever his thoughts, he stood alone on the river bank, watching the threatening gestures of the aroused warriors. Speaking in an undertone, he directed one of his own Indian guides to join him on the shore, there to edge quietly toward the cover of nearby trees.

While the guide was doing this, Alexander scooped up a number of trinkets, including beads, mirrors, and knives, and stuffed them into a bag. Then, after giving quick orders to his other followers, he walked alone a distance downstream. Although he carried his rifle in his right hand, he was relying on the natives' lack of knowledge of firearms. With luck, they would not realize he was armed.

His own Indian, who had slipped into the woods, now covered him as he strolled along. The guide had been told not to fire unless Alexander himself fired first. The other Indian stayed near the canoe with the rest of the party; he continued to call out reassuringly.

Alexander's bold gesture intrigued the natives. They stopped firing arrows to gape at him in wonder. Alexander halted, opened his bag, and showed the trinkets, waving them over his head. Then in pantomime he indicated that he wanted to present gifts. It was futile to call to the natives; they could understand neither his English nor the Indian dialects he spoke.

One by one the curious natives came down to the far bank to peer at him. He continued to gesture, smiling broadly. Then he summoned from the woods the guide who again called to the braves, telling them the stranger was their friend. Alexander himself finally broke his silence; speaking slowly, he assured the Indians that he meant them no harm. His guide translated for him, sentence by sentence.

They conferred, then three of them climbed into a canoe and paddled across the river. Although they were hesitant and shy, Alexander soon won their confidence. He presented each with a knife and string of beads. They were fascinated by the mirrors, but he refused to part with any of those magical objects. His guide, meanwhile, continued to tell the warriors that this astounding stranger wanted nothing from them but friendship.

The three braves were satisfied; they recrossed the river to report to their companions. Again a long conference, then the natives beckoned. Alexander walked slowly back to his boat. He and the guide climbed in, crossed the river and the two parties met.

Alexander passed out gifts with a lavish hand. He was pleased that his guides and the local natives could communicate. Actually their languages were roughly similar even though they lived on opposite sides of the Rocky Mountains. A fire was built now, and the natives offered the newcomers large quantities of salmon, the first fish of this kind that the explorers had eaten.

The natives, Alexander learned, were members of a tribe called Carriers. They had earned this name because the tribe's widows carried for a period of six moons the cremated bones of their husbands in sacks tied around their necks.

There were many Carrier villages in the vicinity, Alexander was told. The warriors were so delighted by his peaceful intentions that they promised to pass the word to their relatives. The explorers would not be attacked in Carrier country.

Alexander asked many questions and received precise replies. The river was very long. It emptied into a great sea or "lake" of salt water. Somewhere near the mouth of the river, the Carriers believed, light-skinned men were building large, substantial houses of wood. The river was a dangerous foe; its current was powerful throughout its entire course. In three places rapids required travelers to make long portages.

The friendly talk was interrupted when a war party in canoes paddled upstream. The newly arrived Indians were surprised to see their brothers sitting around a fire with the strangers; they had been warned by the excited courier to expect a battle. All the war party was armed with spears, stone hatchets, bows and arrows. One warrior, a man in his forties, was obviously the chief; the others spoke to him most respectfully.

Assuming charge at once, he took over the questioning. Why had the strangers come to this part of the world? Where were they going? What was the reason for their journey? Why were they making valuable gifts to his braves while asking nothing in return?

Alexander replied earnestly and at length. Eventually the chief appeared satisfied. He shared a salmon steak with the Scotsman as a gesture of friendship. Alexander, now resuming his own questioning, gleaned some new information. Although the river was long and dangerous, a nearby overland route to the "Lake-whose-waters-made-men-ill-if-they-drank-it" was relatively short. Many tribes used this route to carry to the coast skins of beaver, lynx, bear, marten, and fox; in return they received iron, copper, brass, and large quantities of beads.

The chief denied, too, that pale-skinned strangers were actually building houses on the coast. Instead, he declared, they appeared in boats as large as islands and traded with the coastal tribes.

After everyone had eaten, Alexander conferred with the members of his party. He was tempted, he told them, to take the overland route to the Pacific rather than follow the river. The Carrier's description of the Fraser made him wonder if they could reach the coast in time to return to Fort Athabaska before winter. Of course, even if they traveled by the overland road, they might have to wait until the following spring before crossing the Rocky Mountain barrier. Nevertheless he was willing to take the risk.

None of his subordinates agreed with him. In fact, the *voyageurs* were still anxious to turn back at once. They pointed out that the salvaged lead bars had made only a small quantity of ammunition; furthermore, the guides were poor hunters, often squandering bullets in trying to bring down game. So now the party might indeed starve. It was possible, too, that if they were attacked by a hostile tribe they might not have enough ammunition to protect themselves.

Alexander was entirely confident of his own ability to deal with the natives, and he argued that he carried enough trinkets in the baggage to trade for food. His subordinates were not impressed. He realized he must tread warily or they would abandon the expedition then and there.

Information obtained from Indians, he pointed out, often proved unreliable. Perhaps the overland journey to the coast would require even less than the six days the chief had estimated. Alexander said he would interrogate the Carriers again and then make up his mind.

That night he sat down at the fire with the chief; most of the details he had learned earlier were repeated. But a new element crept into the story. Some distance up the Fraser River, in the direction from which the explorers had come, was a tributary, later to be called the Blackwater, that offered a shorter route to the coast, principally by boat, provided the men traveled in small canoes. It was navigable for a distance of four days' travel; thereafter an overland journey of only two days would take them to their destination.

Alexander stayed awake most of the night, thinking. By dawn he had reached several decisions. Before he could communicate them to anyone, however, the Carrier chief and most of his braves departed, leaving behind two warriors to accompany the expedition as guides. The natives, who had left their own homes hastily, were anxious to return to their families. Therefore they paddled off quickly before Alexander had a chance to tell them of his change in plans.

His own guides, who had been with him from the start of the journey, were out hunting. So no one could act as an interpreter and help him communicate with the two Carriers. Furthermore, he saw no pressing need to tell the natives what he had in mind.

At breakfast he informed his own men that he had decided to retrace his steps to the river that would take them to the coast by a direct route. Speaking eloquently and enthusiastically, he dwelt at length on the ease of the journey awaiting the company. After spending only four days on the water, they would make an easy overland march of two days to the Pacific. There was enough pemmican and parched corn to last for another month, he declared. In addition, the Carrier chief had assured him that the large, pink fish eaten the previous day and again that morning were plentiful. That being so, they would have enough fresh food to sustain them; the better part of their pemmican could be saved for emergencies.

He hoped everyone would decide to go with him, he repeated, but, if necessary, he would proceed alone.

The *voyageurs* responded as they had so often in the past; they agreed to follow him no matter what route he chose. Mackay privately told his superior he believed the shorter route preferable. Bishop was pleased, too. So Alexander decided that he had made the right choice.

One of the Carrier guides wanted to go off to his village now to fetch his hunting and fishing equipment. Alexander consented and, eager to see one of the native communities, offered to accompany the native. His own guides went along too; Mackay, remaining behind with Bishop and the *voyageurs*, was ordered to proceed upstream.

Alexander, the Carrier, and the two Indians from the Peace River country traveled overland through the forests to a small village. The pale-skinned foreigner was welcomed there cordially. The houses Alexander observed were unlike any he had ever seen. Substantial dwellings of wood, their floors and lower walls stood below the surface of the earth in large, rectangular holes dug by the natives. Cancre explained that the natives were warmer in winter because their homes were not completely above ground.

Fresh salmon were grilled on an open fire. Alexander had expected to rejoin his comrades on the Fraser River soon after the meal. But strange, inexplicable things began to happen. The Carrier guide held long, secretive conversations with other residents of the village. Soon the women and children disappeared into the forests of poplar, pine, and birch. The few warriors of the village, formerly amicable, now kept their distance, regarding Alexander with open suspicion tinged with fear.

The Carrier guide was reluctant to offer an explanation.

The grilled salmon was delicious, but Alexander, feeling uncomfortable, ate rapidly. Then he set out again with his own guides and the Carrier brave. The latter raced through the forest at such a rapid pace that everyone was forced to run to keep up with him. The fellow was behaving, Alexander thought, like a man trying to break away and lose himself in the woods.

They reached the banks of the Fraser. Soon after they started upstream, they saw a canoe manned by three Carrier warriors. The natives, catching sight of Alexander, abandoned their boat and fled into the forest. The Carrier guide, openly fearful now, refused to explain his brothers' erratic behavior.

Cancre suggested that the local men might be alarmed because the strangers had changed their plans. Instead of continuing south and west via the Fraser River, the explorers were now going upstream in the opposite direction. Therefore, Cancre said, the Carriers suspected the strangers of treachery.

This reasoning seemed absurd to Alexander. The Carrier chief himself had told of the shorter route to the coast. Nevertheless, Mackenzie was determined now to make his purpose clear to the Carrier guide. At nightfall they encountered two other families of Carriers. Mackay had not reached the point designed as a rendezvous, but Alexander decided not to wait for him before offering the natives an explanation. A fire was made, and Cancre interpreted as he told the natives why he was no longer following the Fraser.

The Indians seemed to accept his explanations. So he believed the matter settled and that night he slept more soundly than usual. When dawn came, he was astonished to find that the two families had vanished. He tried to question the Carrier guide, but the man suddenly panicked. Making no reply, he raced off into the forest, bellowing at the top of his voice.

After the guide vanished, neither of Alexander's own Indians could find him. Then, worried about Mackay and the other members of the expedition, he started downstream again.

After traveling a short distance, he came upon Mackay, Bishop, and the *voyageurs*, all in a state of fatigue. Mackay told a bewildering story. The previous day, soon after starting out, they had encountered a small band of warriors with whom their Carrier guide had held a brief conversation. The warriors had then disappeared, and after that the guide had taken care to keep a considerable distance between his own small canoe and their cumbersome boat.

Early in the afternoon a large war party of angry braves, appearing suddenly from the forest, had launched a determined attack on the strangers. Scores of arrows had been aimed at the men in the clumsy canoe before they could even load their weapons. Then Mackay had fired a single rifle shot, so terrifying the natives that they had vanished again.

After that the explorers had proceeded with great caution, Mackay and Bishop traveling on shore to make certain the *voyageurs* would not be ambushed. Occasionally hearing faint sounds in the woods, they had known they were being watched even though they had seen no one. Afraid that a heavy assault might be launched at any time, they had made camp on a flat, treeless stretch of ground. Even though no one could have approached the spot without being seen, Mackay had decided to take no unnecessary chances. He had not allowed a fire to be built.

The explorers had spent a sleepless night, standing guard with loaded rifles near their baggage and dilapidated canoe. Now, haggard and fearful, their one desire was to return to civilization before they were all murdered.

Alexander refused to budge, even though Mackay and Bishop agreed with the *voyageurs* that it would be sensible to abandon the expedition.

The party traveled a short distance upstream again, halting at an old, abandoned native house of logs. With three of its four walls still standing, Alexander decided to fortify the place. There he planned to await the Carriers and clear up the misunderstanding.

The remaining Carrier guide was watched closely, but soon after camp was made at the abandoned house, he slipped away from his guards and disappeared.

The *voyageurs* and the two Indians accompanying the expedition from the outset made up their minds now to return to their own country, no matter what the leader wanted. Soon after eating a cheerless meal of pemmican and parched corn washed down with river water, they began to load the baggage into the leaky, battered canoe. This was the first time they had ever taken such a step without first receiving a direct order from Alexander or Mackay.

Alexander said nothing at all to them, although the task took a long time. He was hoping that the discipline he had instilled in them would be so effective now that they would not dare to leave on their own initiative. Eventually, however, he realized that they intended to take at face value his often-repeated threat. They would leave for the east without him if he refused to accompany them. Bishop was wavering; even Mackay looked uneasy.

Alexander now made a show of loading and cocking his pistols. Then, walking to the boat, he ordered the *voyageurs* and Indians to unload the baggage.

Not one of the men obeyed.

Alexander suddenly lost his temper. Unless his order was carried out instantly, he roared, he would shoot everyone who resisted his authority.

The surly men slowly unpacked the baggage again.

Alexander, however, was surrounded still by a mutinous company. He was many hundreds of miles from home and deep in territory occupied by hostile warriors. Yet he was determined to reach the Pacific Ocean, no matter how great the odds might be against him.

XV: THE NORTHWEST PASSAGE

ADVERSITY CHALLENGED Alexander Mackenzie; his spirit remained as hard and unyielding as the boulders used to build his makeshift fort on the bank of the Fraser River. Driving his subordinates ruthlessly, he forced them to transform the abandoned house into a strong base capable of withstanding a siege. Scores of boulders were placed around the house in a circle, a palisade was erected outside the ring. The three walls of the house were repaired with logs from trees cut down at the fringe of the forest, and then a fourth wall was raised.

The *voyageurs* and Indian guides remained uncooperative; they obeyed Mackenzie only after he repeated his orders several times.

Alexander, curtly informing them now that he was instituting military discipline, swore he would shoot any man failing to heed a command instantly. The lives of the company depended on co-operation, he insisted; laggards were no better than traitors.

The men took him at his word; they worked furiously.

He supervised their efforts but always carried two loaded, cocked pistols. Once, when a *voyageur* sullenly lay on the ground, he found himself looking into the loaded muzzle of a pistol and changed his mind.

Finally, after work on the fort was completed, the *voyageurs* complained that they did not have enough ammunition to defend themselves. Alexander, though deeply regretting the waste of time, decided that more bullets must be made.

After a huge fire was built, the largest of the iron cooking pots was placed in the center of the blaze. Eventually becoming red-hot and malleable, it was hauled out with green saplings. Then, using an axe, Alexander broke it into smaller pieces and shoved bits of the semi-molten metal into his bullet press. Working all of one day, he converted the pot into several hundred iron bullets. Although his hands were blistered and burned, he gave no sign of the slightest pain or discomfort.

The company was divided now into two groups, one under Alexander, the other under Mackay. They stood guard alternately. A sentinel was stationed a short distance away in the forest. But keeping a single watch for the natives proved so nerve-racking a task that the sentry was changed every hour.

One night a heavy rain virtually completed the destruction of the old canoe. It began to come apart at the seams, but the men were too frightened to go off into the forest and search for the badly needed gum. Similarly, the Indians refused to go hunting. Everyone lived now on the rapidly diminishing supplies of pemmican and parched corn.

Alexander became depressed as he watched precious food stocks dwindling. The men talked of nothing but going home; it seemed unlikely that he would be able to arouse their enthusiasm for the venture again. Actually he could not blame his subordinates for feeling as they did. Realizing that they had reached the end of their endurance, he privately discussed with Mackay the possibility of the lieutenant leading the party back across the Rockies to civilization.

Alexander himself had no intention of quitting. No matter what the outcome, he would continue the journey even if he lost his life in the attempt to reach the coast. Mackay tried to persuade him to change his mind and return with the others, but he refused. He knew he could not live with himself if he failed. Death was preferable to a long life haunted by the knowledge that he had not completed his mission. Never had his spirits sunk as low as they fell during this tense period of waiting.

Then, on the night of June 26, the situation changed. At approximately midnight, the sentinel stationed in the forest reported a rustling noise in the woods. Alexander hurried out to the post but heard nothing. The others were alerted; everyone waited, rifles loaded, for the attack that seemed sure to follow.

Two hours later one of the *voyageurs* caught a glimpse of a gray shape in the wilderness. At first he thought it was a wolf. Then he realized he was looking at a man crawling on his hands and knees. Alexander and Bishop joined the *voyageur*; the three of them crept toward the slow-moving figure.

Alexander was the first to pounce. When he laid hands on the Indian, the native became so frightened that he choked and lost consciousness. After a dram of brandy-wine revived him, he was taken back to the makeshift fort. There the explorers discovered that he was very old, blind, and in frail health.

He was given a meal, which he ate ravenously. Obviously he had touched no food for several days. Gradually his terror abated so that Alexander could question him.

Cancre's analysis proved correct. The Carriers had become panic-stricken after the strangers changed their route. They felt certain that these powerful foreigners must be enemies intending to exterminate the whole tribe. Villages had been evacuated and families had fled deep into the forests, hoping to escape from the wrath of men whose fire-sticks could kill at such great distances.

The old man had been too infirm to travel; instead, he had been hidden in a cave by his wife and given a small amount of food to sustain him. Now hunger had driven him out into the open. He had been searching fruitlessly for provisions, hoping that his family might return before he starved to death.

He made the flat statement that, as long as the strangers remained in the area, none of the Carriers would come home. They would wait in the forests until they were absolutely certain that the foreigners had departed.

Alexander gave the old man plenty to eat and drink. The grateful Indian, reassured by this kindness, offered to accompany the party and render any assistance he could. Alexander accepted at once. Any Indians who saw the old man traveling with the explorers would realize that their fears were groundless. Besides, it was safe to resume the journey, for the Carriers certainly were planning no attack.

The party started out again on June 27, soon after daylight. Progress upstream was painfully slow; the canoe leaked so badly that one man had to spend all his time bailing. The oarsmen exerted every bit of their strength and skill to keep the heavy boat afloat. Tempers were frayed and several violent quarrels erupted. The *voyageurs* were exhausted after paddling only a few miles.

Now Mackenzie realized that a new canoe must be made immediately. Fortunately, the old Indian, grateful for the gentle consideration he had received, told Alexander of a grassy, heavily wooded island where all the raw materials for a new boat could be found.

The *voyageurs* were still in such low spirits that they wanted to halt; Alexander insisted they continue. And at last, shortly before sundown, they came to the island. Camp was pitched, and early the next morning everyone went in search of bark and *watape*, gum and strong, flexible wood for the framework.

They found everything they needed except gum. The new canoe began to take shape.

At Mackay's suggestion, the men took enough gum from the old canoe to waterproof the seams. But the *voyageurs* were still grumbling, and Alexander finally lost all patience. He lectured them severely, calling them cowards and suggesting that, if they still insisted on returning home, they make two canoes instead of one. Then he himself could resume his journey to the Pacific and they could go back to civilization. He demanded that all who intended to quit the party step forward.

A tense silence followed; nobody moved.

Work was then resumed on the new canoe. Before the task was completed, a small boat beached on the island, and the younger of the Carrier guides approached. From his hiding place in the forest, he had seen the old man with the party and, feeling ashamed of himself, had returned to offer his services once again. The attitude of the old man now helped further to restore the guide's confidence.

In an attempt to save face, he insisted that he had not shared the fright of many of his fellow Carriers. He had gone off because his brother-in-law had returned from a journey to the coast with an iron axe, obtained in exchange for a dressed moose skin. Alexander, examining the axe, saw that it was indeed made of iron. Here was fresh proof that the expedition was not far from the Pacific where white traders were operating.

The return of the guide raised the morale of the *voyageurs*; they sang as they launched the new canoe. It was stronger, lighter, and far easier to handle than their battered craft had been even when new. The Peace River Indians went hunting now in the mainland forest. Displaying greater energy than they had shown in many days, they returned with an elk.

That night the party ate fresh meat. Alexander gave every man a double ration of rum; everyone enjoyed the holiday atmosphere.

Early the next morning, the old man asked to be put ashore on the mainland. Certain his relatives would come for him soon, he was not afraid of being left alone now. Nevertheless, Alexander gave him several pounds of pemmican.

The young Carrier warrior went ahead to notify any Indians he met that the strangers were friendly. Neither Alexander nor Mackay felt any confidence in him, however. They feared he would disappear again. Western Indians, they had found, were even less reliable than those east of the Rockies.

With the new canoe, the party made good progress, even though they were working upstream against a strong current. A heavy rain fell, drenching everyone to the skin. The mood of the men had changed, however, and no one protested. Swarms of mosquitoes, deer flies, and sand flies appeared to plague the explorers, too, but they endured such discomforts cheerfully. Alexander took advantage of the men's improved spirits by announcing that henceforth, because of a shortage of food supplies, they would eat only two meals a day. He softened the blow by issuing an extra ration of rum.

At ten o'clock on the morning of July 3, the explorers reached the spot already described by the Carriers. Here the small river which flowed toward the west met the Fraser. Alexander called this stream the West Road River — later it would be known as the Blackwater.

In mid-afternoon several small canoes swept down the Fraser. Leading the flotilla was the guide, resplendent in a gaudy cape of beaver daubed with paints of many colors. He was accompanied by six of his relatives, all of them eager to go with the strangers.

Now the Carriers preceded the main party, but Alexander still mistrusted them. He decided to send along Mackay and Bishop, hoping they would prevent the Indians from deserting.

The West Road River soon proved unsuitable for navigation. The Carrier chief had exaggerated in saying that small canoes could travel down its length for several days. In some places it was only a few yards wide, the bottom was strewn with sharp rocks, and the water was shallow. Certainly the explorers' new canoe was far too large for passage here.

So Alexander decided the party would travel overland to the coast. The expedition carried far too much baggage to be hauled to the Pacific on the men's backs, so Alexander waited until Mackay, Bishop, and the Carriers had gone. Then he ordered two large holes dug. In one, he buried a ninety-pound bag of pemmican, two of wild rice, and a keg of gunpowder. In the other, the men hid two bags of pemmican, two of parched corn, and another containing various trading items to be used on the homeward journey.

The canoe itself was taken some distance from the path the natives had worn through the forest. Balanced between two dead logs, it was carefully covered with thick, leafy branches as a protection from the elements and from marauding natives. The rest of the supplies to be left behind, mainly cumbersome items of hardware, was placed in a hollow square fashioned of green logs and covered with leafy branches. All footprints and other signs leading to the spot were then eliminated.

But even after these reductions, the cargo the men intended to take with them was formidable. Alexander made a careful list of what he and the men would carry:

4 bags of pemmican of 90 pounds each

1 case of scientific instruments

2 packs of trinkets and trading goods of 90 pounds each

1 90-pound pack of ammunition

In addition, the men were burdened by their weapons, personal ammunition and gunpowder, blankets and toilet articles, and spare clothing. In all, nearly one thousand pounds of supplies had to be divided among the party. The two Peace River Indians just carried their own rifles and two half-pack bags of pemmican which they loathed and would have abandoned by the wayside had they dared.

So now, by using his instruments and following the descriptions of the Pacific coast in Captain Cook's books, Alexander estimated privately that the party must march approximately three hundred miles before reaching its destination. And, unless fresh game was shot or food obtained from the natives, the men would be restricted to two meals a day.

The *voyageurs* would be carrying more than one hundred pounds of cargo apiece. Alexander himself took seventy pounds of equipment and, in addition, elected to carry his clumsy twenty-pound telescope as well as his precious books.

Each man made careful personal preparation for the overland journey. Resin was collected, the explorers rubbing quantities of it on the soles of their feet to harden them. Then they massaged their legs with the juice of fir trees, a custom of the Algonquin Indians of the eastern seaboard. These Indians did this just before setting out on long marches. Strenuous attempts were made as well to find a deer or elk, since the boiled blood of wild animals was supposed to give a man added strength. Unfortunately game remained scarce.

Alexander hurriedly brought his notebooks up to date. He was tempted to let them eat an extra meal, but the scarcity of food hardened his resolve.

The overland march began at noon on July 4. The explorers, led by their Carrier guides, made their way through a forest in full leaf, toiling up a long slope toward a plateau.

Alexander scarcely felt the weight on his back. Each step brought him closer to the realization of the dream that had challenged mankind for almost three hundred years.

XVI: THE LAND OF PLENTY

THE EXPLORERS found themselves in a world unlike any they had ever known. The farther west they marched, the more astonished they became. The trees in the forests were enormous, one mammoth cedar being larger than a dozen maples in the woods that lined the St. Lawrence River. Native villages appeared everywhere; the Indians lived in solid, permanent dwellings. Dressed from head to toe in sturdy clothing, they seemed without exception well fed. Salmon was king in this realm. The abundance of fish overwhelmed men who had subsisted for so long on greasy pemmican.

But Alexander saw something he considered vastly more important than all these wonders. In a small village on the shore of a lake, he caught sight of glittering coins hanging from the earlobes of a little girl. He was elated when he found they were copper halfpennies. One was English and bore the likeness of King George III; the other was American and had been minted in the state of Massachusetts in 1787. The copper was still shiny. Although the child's parents would tell Alexander nothing about where the coins came from, he thought they must have been given to natives on the coast in a recent trading operation.

Since the sea seemed near at hand at last, Mackenzie increased the pace of the march. The men, sharing his excitement, made their way cheerfully across rough terrain, undeterred by underbrush, hills, or steep ravines.

The explorers marched seventeen miles one day, twenty-two another, then twenty-five. Everywhere Indians they encountered said they would reach the sea "soon." When pressed for a more accurate estimate, the natives always repeated that the ocean could be reached in an eight-day march. But after spending four long days on the trail, carrying heavy packs, the men became exasperated. The *voyageurs* began to wonder if the Pacific really existed.

Guides hired along the way proved unreliable. Warriors eagerly accepted the promise of gifts, but Alexander's pace soon exhausted them. More often than not, a brave disappeared shortly after he had joined the party.

Only Alexander seemed aware of the tree-covered hills, picturesque lakes, and the mint and mustard plants growing in profusion on their banks. His companions, however, were in no mood to enjoy the scenery.

At least, no one went hungry. There was salmon in abundance in every village, every hamlet, and the natives willingly sold the strangers as much as Alexander wanted to buy. Unfortunately, few of the fish were fresh, and those that had been smoked and dried the previous season were tasteless. But anything was better than pemmican.

Then, one morning, an unexpected obstacle appeared. A range of snow-covered mountains loomed ahead. The latest group of local guides vanished; the explorers were alone now, on foot, in a strange, uncharted wilderness.

Alexander, refusing to abandon hope, continued to lead his men toward the southwest. His faith and patience were rewarded at last when he learned from the natives of a village that the "Bitter Sea" was visible from the mountain heights.

Three Indian warriors, a father and his two sons, offered to act as guides, but Alexander was forced to hesitate. He literally could not afford to feed three additional mouths.

The middle-aged Indian waved aside his fears. All interior natives, he said, were accustomed to living on herbs and on the glutinous inside lining of tree barks. He took the explorers out into the woods to illustrate what he meant. Using a thin, razor-shaped piece of bone that hung on a thong from his waist, he stripped the bark of the nearest tree and began to eat.

Alexander tasted the substance; he found it sweet, clammy, and somewhat offensive. The natives were surprised that he did not enjoy the bark lining, for they considered it a great delicacy.

In any event, all three Indians agreed to accompany the expedition. The march was resumed at once. They walked rapidly toward the mountains, climbed one hill after another and spurred on by the guide's prediction that they would reach the range in a day or two and cross it in one more.

That afternoon they came to a swift-flowing river; Alexander believed it to be a hitherto undiscovered branch of the Fraser. Actually it was the Blackwater, but much larger and stronger here than he had seen it in other places up to that time. The local Indians informed him that, at other seasons, this river was filled with salmon.

The total lack of game was puzzling, for the grassy slopes and heavy, leafy woods seemed ideally suited for wild life. Alexander, thinking in terms of the future, decided to bury some pemmican for the return journey. Because he could spare very little, he cached only a forty-five-pound bag. Extra precautions were needed in this area where food seemed to be so scarce, so a fire was burned over the covered hole to disguise the spot.

Rain fell, but the party continued without rest. When they came to a river too wide to be forded on foot, a raft was made. They had approached once more the meandering Blackwater, but this they did not know. A short time later, from the crest of a high hill, they saw in the distance a chain of seven lakes.

Their guides informed them that, unfortunately, there were no fish in the lakes just then.

Soon after the sun rose on July 14, the party caught a glimpse of a large river from the top of another hill. This stream in later years would become known as the Dean River. The middle-aged guide, familiar with the whole territory, told Alexander that the bed of the river was free of rocks so that the stream was navigable by canoe.

Shortly after noon, a large group of natives camped beside the trail gave the explorers a boisterous welcome, mistaking them for fellow Indians. The warriors and squaws found it hard to believe that these heavily suntanned, tattered human beings were actually pale-skinned foreigners like those who sailed up and down the coast in huge wooden canoes. Alexander privately decided that, just before reaching the Pacific, he and his men must improve their appearance.

Since the Indians were traveling with more than enough food, they offered the explorers dried salmon of excellent quality, beans, and a variety of dried corn with tiny kernels. To Alexander's astonishment, the Indians refused payment for the supplies. He insisted, however, on giving everyone a gift.

The two groups now agreed to travel together. The explorers did not protest when the Indians informed them that, because of the women and children, three days would be required to reach the coast. The end of the long trail was within reach at last. The tired *voyageurs*, accustomed to spending the better part of their time riding in canoes, were not anxious to hike rapidly. Actually, the Indians' concept of a slow march was curious, for, between that afternoon and the next, more than twenty miles were covered.

Then Alexander received an unexpected blow. His volatile new friends told him they had changed their minds. They now planned to follow the course of a small river taking them near to the sea but not actually to it. As a matter of fact, they planned to follow what is now known as the Salmon River to the Dean Channel, an inlet of the Pacific. If Alexander had accompanied them, he would have reached the ocean far more quickly. Unfortunately, too many interpreters spoiled communications. The Indians assumed he wanted to make his way to the sea by a more southerly route, and Mackenzie believed they were not intending to camp on the shores of the Pacific.

One of the warriors suggested, however, that if the strangers would tarry on the road for another night, he would prepare a great delicacy for them as a parting gift. Alexander agreed. The brave took a large number of salmon roes from a bag, bruised them between his fingers, and placed them in water to soak. Then he made a large fire to heat stones.

In the meantime his squaw gathered large handfuls of dry grass. Using them as a primitive form of sieve, she squeezed the roes through the tangled mass of blades. Then she filled a large kettle with water, placing the roes inside. When the stones were very hot, she threw a few into the kettle, gradually adding others until the water began to boil. From time to time she tossed others into the pot to keep the water boiling. She and her husband took turns stirring the contents vigorously. Gradually the roes, grass, and water assumed the consistency of a rough, thick paste. Finally the stones were removed and, as a last touch, the dish was seasoned with approximately one pint of strong, rancid fish oil.

The odor of this strange dish sickened Alexander before he had even tasted the concoction. But his men were so hungry they ate every bite. Boiled roes of salmon, he noted, were quite palatable when unadulterated by the foul-smelling oil.

Fortified by this questionable breakfast, the explorers set out again, led by their new guides. They forded the Salmon River at a spot where the water was only knee-deep, then climbed up into the mountains. The guides led them toward the passes that would take them to the western slopes. There they would find the river pointing the way to the Pacific.

The crossing of this last barrier proved difficult. On Wednesday, July 17, the party reached the heights of the mountain pass. They found the hard-packed snow underfoot as stiff and unyielding as solid rock. A heavy storm suddenly blew up, winds tore at the travelers, and an avalanche of hail fell on them. The men were so numbed that walking became agonizing, but they did not dare to halt. The peaks to the north and south disappeared behind black clouds; the party groped its way forward fearfully.

At last the weather cleared sufficiently for them to see an enormous mountain directly ahead. Snow covered its peak. The explorers were dismayed, thinking they would be forced to climb it. But their guides led them along a narrow path taking them past the river rather than over it. And that afternoon the Peace River Indians, spurred by hunger became sufficiently energetic to shoot a caribou doe.

The valley that sloped down toward the ocean was directly ahead now. Alexander had no intention of staggering to its shores looking like a tattered scarecrow. Every cooking pot was filled with water and heated. He bathed carefully, shaved, and donned clean clothes saved for the occasion. The other members of the party followed his example. Soon all were prepared to make the descent looking like representatives of the civilized world.

The next morning they moved down rapidly from the heights. Standing on the edge of a precipice, the explorers saw the westward-flowing river. On its banks was a large native village. The guides went ahead to prepare the inhabitants for the arrival of the strangers, while the explorers made their way through hills covered with fine stands of pine, hemlock, birch, and spruce. In about two hours they reached the valley where the forest was dense. Alexander was particularly impressed by the cedar trees; they were the largest and tallest he had ever seen.

At the village itself, an elderly chief of the Salish tribe greeted the strangers with great ceremony, clasping each by the shoulders and making a speech of welcome. Squaws were working before a large fire. The visitors were conducted to an open platform of cedar that extended beyond the edge of the house. Mats of cedar bark were placed before them, then the squaws appeared with large, roasted salmon steaks.

The explorers ate hungrily, but Alexander, remembering his manners, took his time, cutting and spearing each bite of meat with his knife. A second course was served. The visitors hesitated when they saw a creamy, pink substance in gourds. It proved to be whipped salmon eggs which they found delicious. Then, to their surprise, they were given a third course — gooseberries flavored with sorrel. Alexander correctly assumed that the chief was giving a feast in his honor. The visitors were eating the favorite dishes of the Salish.

After the women and children retired to parts unknown, the explorers were invited to sleep in the house where a fire had been prepared for their comfort on a stone hearth. The walls were lined with planks raised a few inches from the ground and covered with tender boughs. These couches gave the weary travelers the softest beds they had enjoyed on their entire journey. Even Alexander, cutting short his work on his notebooks after the others had retired, slept soundly.

The next morning he found himself in the midst of the most advanced, cultivated Indian civilization he had ever encountered. The meat of wild mountain goats was served for breakfast. His hosts told him that large herds of goats grazed in the nearby hills. He noted, however, that only the chief and his male relatives ate the meat. The breakfast of the other natives consisted entirely of fish. Animal flesh, it seemed, was forbidden food for most members of the tribe. This dietary law was strictly observed.

Salmon and cedar were indeed king and queen here, and the aristocrats of the Salish had become wealthy and powerful. A dam had been built across the river, a feat requiring great skill and imagination. Only primitive tools had been used. Below the dam were salmon traps in which, each year, many thousands of fish were caught. These traps were the exclusive property of the chief; he doled out fish to his subjects as he saw fit. This made him a man to be feared and respected by his people.

Alexander tried in vain to obtain some raw salmon to take on the journey. The chief willingly gave him all the cooked fish he could carry and filled several bags with berries and containers of fish oil. But after great hesitation, he explained that the taboos of the tribe strictly prohibited any but true believers from touching raw salmon. The gods of the fish were potent, the chief said. If he violated their commands, the fish would leave the river for other waters and the Salish people would starve.

There seemed to be no taboos, however, prohibiting the use of the huge, plentiful cedar trees. Virtually all houses were made of this wood, and only the slaves — warriors of other tribes captured in war — lived in mud huts. The Salish displayed great ingenuity in their architecture; even the roofs of their houses were fashioned of cedar shingles.

The outer bark of the trees made sturdy, supple rope; twisted, dried roots were utilized as fire-lighting spills which the natives called "traveling fire." The inner bark was a substitute for cloth, and the women wove it to make clothing for themselves and their children. The explorers marveled at the softness of the fabric. This inner bark produced also bedding and the strange helmets fastened to the heads of infants.

Virtually all household utensils were made of cedar, and the explorers saw kettles and pots, bowls and platters, treasure chests and even coffins of this wood. War canoes were fashioned from cedar, watertight baskets were woven of split cedar roots, and beautiful ceremonial masks for religious services were carved from cedar blocks.

The Salish also utilized carved cedar to make impressive totem poles. These poles were intricately worked — some crudely done, others showing remarkable, if stylized, artistic talent. Most were painted in many colors with dyes obtained from the roots of plants and from berries. On them were inscribed the histories of great chiefs, of families, and even of whole villages.

Cedar had many other uses, too. The lining of the soft inner bark became a food supplement. Strangely, only the aristocrats — that is, the chiefs and their relatives — and property owners were permitted to eat this substance. Supposedly it gave a man great courage. Prisoners of war, forced to work as slaves, were not permitted to touch it.

All of the Salish males seemed to be adept at carving. The prows of their fishing boats and war canoes bore testimony to their skill. Nowhere had Alexander seen squaws who were more expert weavers or whose tastes in the blending of colors more nearly approximated those of civilized women. All in all, he felt so completely at home with these natives that he dared to hope his troubles were at an end.

XVII: THE PACIFIC OCEAN

IGNORANCE OF THE CUSTOMS and superstitions of the Indians living near the Pacific now jeopardized the lives of the explorers. Alexander Mackenzie, relaxing for the first time in many weeks, had no idea that he and his men were innocently upsetting taboos and arousing the open hatred of the Salish and their neighbors, the Bella Coola.

On the morning of July 18, his hosts were still convivial, food was plentiful, and all his men were rested. He spent a long time watching the Indians catching salmon, carefully inspecting the ponds into which the fish were forced by dams and paying particular attention to the Salish nets. These contraptions made of split roots of cedar were so ingenious that he wanted one to keep, hoping later to present it to Cambridge University. But the Indians said they had none to spare.

Perhaps the Scotsman's habit of taking extensive notes aroused the suspicion of his hosts. Or perhaps, as Mackay later thought, the explorer's desire to purchase a canoe was responsible. Certainly every member of the party was anxious to leave, for the natives indicated that the Pacific was no more than thirty miles away. With luck, they could travel to the coast in a single day. With delays, they could complete their long journey easily in two.

The chief of the Salish insisted on giving them another banquet at noon. They dined royally on large steaks of roasted salmon and huge bowls of gooseberries, raspberries, and huckleberries.

But Alexander's request for one or more canoes was rejected with surprising brusqueness. Instead, the chief offered to send the party downstream in two of his own canoes manned by eight Salish braves. Alexander accepted with alacrity, realizing that the Indians wanted to keep his men under constant surveillance. This belief was confirmed when the chief added that they would not need to buy salmon of any kind, even cooked fish, because they would reach the next inhabited place, called the Great Village, after only a short journey.

Suddenly now the hospitable chief made it plain that he wanted to be rid of his guests. The explorers' canoes were carried down to the water and farewell ceremonies were curtailed. Alexander's Peace River guides could not explain the very definite change in the attitude of the Salish.

The current was swift; the two canoes sped downstream. There was considerable traffic on the stream, with large numbers of Indians traveling in both directions. The *voyageurs* were impressed by the ease with which the natives handled their craft. Alexander had always believed that *voyageurs* were the best canoemen on earth, but now he had to revise his estimates. The *voyageurs* themselves conceded that the natives were their peers.

After about two and one-half hours, the strangers were asked to land and walk through a forest of towering cedar trees to the Great Village. Several of the Salish oarsmen hurried ahead to notify the inhabitants that strangers were coming; others remained close to the explorers. All apparently had been instructed not to let the foreigners wander by themselves through the countryside.

The explorers, presently coming out into the open, caught a glimpse of many large cedar buildings directly ahead. Suddenly several dozen warriors ran out of the houses, screaming and shouting, and armed with bows and arrows, iron-tipped spears, and heavy axes of stone. Couriers raced from house to house, alerting the inhabitants. The women and children, who had been circulating in a large dusty square, ran indoors now.

A number of warriors notched arrows in their bows, others ran toward the strangers brandishing spears. Evidently the natives intended to attack in force. The explorers immediately raised their rifles.

But Alexander sensed that a battle would be ruinous to his hopes. He could defeat the Indians in a single fight, but, in doing so, he would make enemies of all the natives in this heavily populated area. As a result his men would have to keep defending themselves constantly, both on the journey to the sea and on their return.

So he shouted a command and his subordinates reluctantly lowered their weapons. Then, handing his own rifle to Mackay, he walked alone and unarmed into the milling crowd of excited natives. They stared at him, stunned by his courage.

But now an old man, shoving aside the braves, broke through the crowd to embrace Alexander with affection. He, in turn, was pushed aside by a younger man, his son, who also embraced the Scotsman. This gesture, as Alexander soon learned, was a sign of friendship and trust. The chief and his son belonged to the Bella Coola nation, a tribe of Indians who lived on the stream down which the party had been traveling.

The attitude of the warriors changed now, too. All the explorers were embraced. The throng of Indians pressed so close to the strangers that no one could move. Mackay and Bishop feared that the volatile natives might suddenly change their attitude once again, yet Alexander himself remained calm and apparently unflustered, although later he confessed to his lieutenant that he had passed a few uncomfortable moments.

The crowd moved aside now to let a tall warrior in a splendid cape of sea otter approach the strangers. One of the Salish muttered that he was the eldest son of the Bella Coola chief, information Cancre quickly translated. Alexander took several steps forward, smiling and extending his right hand.

The crown prince of the Bella Coola halted, looked him up and down, then broke the thong holding his cape. Removing the cloak, he flung it around Alexander's shoulders. The warriors began to cavort and sing. The crisis was at an end. That night the chief and his son gave another banquet for the explorers, who again slept on comfortable pine boughs.

The next morning Alexander was paid a high compliment: he was asked to treat the dying youngest son of the chief. All the Scotsman could do was to try to ease his pain.

The chief then showed the visitors his treasures, including various utensils of iron obtained from English or Russian coastal traders.

Alexander was deeply moved when the chief displayed a magnificent canoe capable of holding forty men. Years earlier, the chief said, he had gone to sea in the vessel and had seen two large ships manned by pale-skinned foreigners. They had treated him with great kindness. Those foreigners, Alexander felt certain, must have been members of Captain Cook's expedition. The canoe, forty-five feet long, was made of a hollowed cedar log. It was painted a glossy black and decorated with white drawings of fish. The gunwales, both fore and aft, were inlaid with the teeth of sea otters. Alexander was convinced that this was the very boat that Cook had described as being "adorned with human teeth." For the teeth of the sea otters, Alexander discovered on close examination, resembled those of people.

Yet in spite of the chief's friendliness, he was reluctant to let the strangers continue to the coast. Several times Alexander asked him for boats and guides, but the Bella Coola kept procrastinating, uneasily changing the subject and, finally, falling glumly silent. Alexander, prepared to continue without help now if necessary, produced his scientific instruments to measure the altitude above sea level. The natives begged him to put away the instruments; they were certain that the gods of the salmon would take offense. But the Scotsman's patience was exhausted; he ignored the exhortations.

At once the chief produced both canoes and guides. Alexander was all ready to depart when he discovered that his personal axe, a Sheffield-made tool of steel, had vanished. He demanded its return, but the chief, his sons, and the other warriors of the nation only looked at him with blank, innocent faces.

If he permitted the theft to go unpardoned, most of the expedition's baggage would undoubtedly disappear in the next few days. Alexander jumped onto a rock, drew his pistol, and announced that he would not depart until the axe was returned. His own men became apprehensive, the natives muttered to each other. The situation was growing increasingly tense.

Alexander, always calm in an emergency, aimed his pistol at a large salmon drying on a line and pulled the trigger. The fish fell apart. The warriors were panic-stricken; they raced up and down the waterfront screaming. The chief threw himself on the ground and buried his head under his sea-otter cloak. His arms and legs grew rigid with fright. Only the crown prince kept his head; he suddenly "found" the axe beneath his father's canoe.

Having established a principle to his satisfaction, Alexander was now ready to leave. He was given canoes and native oarsmen now, for the inhabitants were eager to see him on his way.

Although the river was almost one continuous rapid, the native paddlers were marvelously adroit. The explorers sped downstream past dwellings like those they had seen in the villages. Gradually the voyage became more difficult as the strong current rushed toward the Pacific through narrow channels. At last the explorers and their guides came to a waterfall where they were forced to make a portage. The party walked down a trail through the woods to still another village. Night had come; the visitors were warmly received here.

From his hosts, Alexander learned something of the utmost importance. Only a month earlier, they told him, a group of pale-skinned men had appeared at the village in boats lowered from a huge vessel of wood. Alexander, having learned in London something about the exploration plans of various countries, assumed that the expedition must be British. Captain George Vancouver of the Royal Navy, a veteran seaman who had gone with Cook on two expeditions and who had also served under Admiral Rodney, had been searching the Pacific coast for a river large enough to be followed across the continent on an overland journey. Vancouver had also been instructed to plant the Union Jack wherever he saw fit. Great Britain was anxious to dispose of Spain's claim to the region later to be known as British Columbia.

The Indians further revealed that the men in the huge wooden ship had sailed off along the coast toward the south; Alexander assumed from this that Vancouver had gone in the direction of the Spanish Californias which the British called New Albion. The chance of meeting Vancouver somewhere along the coast, therefore, was slight, but Alexander was determined to pursue his fellow countryman if the opportunity presented itself. For this purpose he obtained a hollowed cedar canoe from the local natives. His provisions, however, were so low now as to have become virtually non-existent. None of the coastal Indians would sell him food. All he carried at this point was twenty pounds of pemmican, sixteen of rice, and six of corn flour. In brief, he had only enough supplies to feed his men for two days.

Nevertheless, he took heart the following morning; he could see, from the raised house where he had slept, an inlet of the ocean. The Bella Coola River emptied into it. In years to come, that inlet was to be known as the North Bentinck Arm of Dean Channel. A bay lay directly ahead, so Alexander felt certain that before sundown he would actually reach the coast. After marking the date, July 20, in his notebook, he was prepared to start at seven o'clock in the morning.

But the guides who had accompanied him from the Great Village refused to go any farther. They argued that he had wanted to be taken to the sea, and that it was now within sight. Nothing would persuade them to continue, so Alexander determined to go on alone. He and his men started off at eight o'clock in the dugout, their sail hoisted.

The tide was out; seaweed littered the beach on both sides of the channel. The strong odor of bracing salt filled the air. Suddenly a head wind sprang up, forcing the *voyageurs* to use their paddles.

The company came soon to a bay filled with sea otters and porpoises. High on a rock to the north, a white-headed eagle perched; small gulls circled overhead, and several ducks appeared on a little island in the bay.

Game seemed so plentiful that the hunters took their time loading their rifles. This was a mistake because the winds became stronger and a heavy fog blew in from the ocean. It soon became impossible to see more than a few feet ahead of the dugout canoe. Then the tide roared in, and the swell was so strong that by mid-afternoon the company was forced to land at a small cove.

The tide continued to rise, soaring a total of fifteen feet in all. The explorers scrambled to higher ground, dragging with them their baggage and the canoe. Eleven hungry men were marooned now on a thin crescent of beach lying at the edge of a forest of low pines and heavy underbrush. In spite of the fog, Alexander sent most of the company hunting; they returned with a lone porcupine which they roasted. The company named the spot Porcupine Cove; it was later changed to Green Bay.

Mackay was so hungry that he gathered and roasted large quantities of mussels, proclaiming them delicious. Only Alexander joined him in eating them, however. The others, being unfamiliar with shellfish, feared that the strange little creatures in the purple shells might be poisonous.

Alexander wanted to take a precise observation of latitude and longitude now, but he needed a clear sky. His men were so hungry that they thought of nothing but going home. However, the leader's will prevailed, as usual. On the morning of July 21, the party continued down one of the many channels leading toward the sea. They had gone only a short distance when they encountered fifteen Indians traveling in three canoes. Both parties went ashore to converse.

The attitude of these natives was different from any previously encountered. The braves viewed the possessions of the explorers with indifference and disdain. The leader of the party, an arrogant, unfriendly warrior, informed Alexander that a large wooden ship filled with pale-faced men had sailed into the bay recently. The chief of the pale-skinned men, whom the brave called "Macubah" — an obvious reference to Vancouver — had fired a pistol at him. And another member of the party, the native declared, had struck him on the back with the flat of a sword.

After telling of these misadventures, the brave demanded that Alexander carry him to a narrow, nearby channel which led to his own village. Alexander wanted to reject the request but thought it prudent to agree. On the brief voyage, the warrior made a nuisance of himself. First, he asked to see all the explorers' belongings. Then he insisted on receiving Alexander's hat, handkerchief, knife, boots, and pistols as gifts. When Alexander refused to grant him any of these things, he repeated, ominously, that Macubah had fired at him. Next he declared his intention of getting revenge at the expense of other pale-skinned foreigners.

When they reached the channel, Alexander was glad to be rid of the man, but soon discovered that his party was now being followed by ten canoes containing anywhere from three to six Indians each. In all, he estimated, fifty braves were in the party. The fog lifted temporarily. When Mackenzie sighted a rock on which some sheds were standing, he headed toward it, urging the *voyageurs* to row with all possible speed.

They hoped the spot had been one used by Vancouver. It turned out to be all that was left of an abandoned Indian village. Fortunately, however, the rocky promontory was so small that no more than thirty men could crowd onto it. The canoes filled with warriors were drifting closer now. The explorers prepared to defend themselves.

The Indians in the three leading canoes ventured closer to the rock; they seemed spoiling for a fight. Their companions in the other boats, however, kept urging the foreigners to visit their village. They were so insistent that Alexander thought they intended foul play. Displaying great patience, he gently but firmly declined their invitation.

His fear was confirmed when he saw that the troublemaker had reappeared. This surly man was seated in one of the canoes, goading on his companions. Alexander pretended not to see the fellow, but ordered his subordinates to allow none of the natives to come ashore. Several braves now became involved in a long dispute with Mackay, insisting they could land where they pleased. The clerk lacked Mackenzie's patience. He was so annoyed that he raised his rifle. The warriors then decided to leave. Obviously they understood and respected the power of firearms.

A short time later seven middle-aged Indian traders appeared at the rock in another canoe. Heavy-set men, dressed with great care in leather trousers and shirts, they announced that they had engaged in barter with Macubah and his men. They were prepared to do the same with Mackenzie's party. Alexander, believing them to be relatively harmless, agreed that they might land for a short time.

After the Indians had gone, a fire was lighted, fishing nets were cast, and the party settled down for the evening. Within a short time a number of fish were hauled ashore and roasted. Then, unexpectedly, the weather cleared. The moon and stars appeared, and Alexander climbed to the summit of the rock.

The men followed him. No one spoke. Off to the southwest beyond a point of land, the ocean itself could be seen. As a beam of silver moonlight played on the blue-black waters, Alexander held his hands over his eyes for a moment.

At last, after enduring endless hardships, dangers, and near brushes with death, he and his men had fulfilled the dream of the civilized nations of Europe and of the New World. They had found the overland northwest passage across North America, and they stood now at the edge of the Pacific.

XVIII: SURVIVAL OF THE STRONG

ALEXANDER MACKENZIE and his band found it difficult now to celebrate their triumph. Thousands of miles from their own safe, familiar world and with food supplies virtually exhausted, they were in danger of being attacked by hostile, belligerent Indians. Because their supplies of rum and brandy wine had been buried on the trail, they could not even toast each other in any liquid stronger than water.

Alexander himself, quickly recovering his emotional stability, realized that his company badly needed help. Captain Vancouver might just possibly be lingering somewhere in the area off the coast. Since he carried vast quantities of food, ammunition, gunpowder, and other supplies on his ships, Alexander was determined to make every effort to find him.

Mackay, Bishop, and two of the *voyageurs* immediately started south in the dugout canoe, traveling under full sail. They were instructed not to tarry; when they returned, they would be expected to rejoin the main party on the overland trail. If Vancouver should be found, Alexander would then retrace his steps to the seacoast. If Mackay's group did not locate the captain, by the time the bad news reached them the main party would at least be well started on their journey home.

Mackay's voyage was extraordinary. He sailed south along the coast of what is now British Columbia in a hollowed cedar-log boat about thirty-five or forty feet long. Occasionally he and his companions went ashore to shoot game; both venison and elk were plentiful in the region.

The four explorers failed to recognize the channel at the northern end of what is now Vancouver Island, and later a fog prevented them from seeing the channel at the southern end. They went ashore a number of times on the coast of what later became the state of Washington. These brief halts were used in the nineteenth century by Great Britain to substantiate her claim to the region; Mackay, a British subject and the commander of the party, had been the first to set foot on this soil. Bishop, of course, was an American citizen. His presence in the landing party bolstered the claim of the United States to the area.

Such boundary disputes were, however, far from the minds of the four men searching for Captain Vancouver. Their one object was to sail south as quickly as possible, then rejoin their comrades as soon as they could. They worked and slept in shifts, spending virtually all their time on the water. In his report to Alexander, Mackay estimated that a minimum of twenty-one hours out of every twenty-four was spent under sail.

The little group abandoned its search some distance north of the Columbia River, now marking the border between the states of Washington and Oregon. The river was known to exist, for it had been reported by a number of explorers sailing up and down the Pacific coast of the continent. But its exact location was unknown; for some time, Mackenzie actually believed that the Fraser was the Columbia.

Mackay and his companions cared nothing about charting the coastline, finding rivers, or locating mountain ranges. They were seeking the help of a high-ranking officer in the Royal Navy. When they were unable to find any trace of him, they turned north again.

Mackay observed that the terrain was heavily wooded and hilly. Most of the trees he identified were fir and pine, spruce and cedar and hemlock. In some places the forests were even larger and the trees taller than any seen by the main party in its travels.

Two groups of Indians appeared when the men went ashore, but both fled before they could be questioned.

Mackay, fishing in a small but swift-running river, had the good fortune to catch a salmon similar to those found farther north. Moreover, he and his companions came upon an abundance of game. In spite of the long, grueling hours spent in the tiny boat, the four men ate heartily.

Meanwhile Alexander and his larger group did not fare so well. After Mackay departed, Alexander immediately sent one of the Peace River warriors inland to the Great Village to ask help from the crown prince of the tribe. The Indian was to be promised a liberal reward if he would come for Mackenzie's party in a canoe and act as a guide for the homeward trek.

Having done everything in his power to summon aid, Alexander spent the rest of the night making, checking, and rechecking astronomical observations. He was anxious to record the precise latitude and longitude of the spot where he had reached the Pacific. He calculated the position as 128° 2' west of Greenwich and 52° 21' 10" north. His reckoning was surprisingly good, considering the inaccuracy of eighteenth century instruments and his own relative lack of experience. Only recently has Alexander's finding been found to have been about thirty miles too far to the west.

The night passed quietly, and on the morning of July 23, the Peace River guide appeared from the Great Village with the crown prince, accompanied by several warriors in two canoes. The guide had located them camping on the banks of the lower Bella Coola and persuaded them to join the explorers.

Before heading east, Alexander took still more observations to make a check of his earlier calculations. Then he obtained some vermilion from the Indians, mixed it with a little grease, and wrote on the southeast face of the rock: ALEXANDER MACKENZIE, FROM CANADA BY LAND, THE 22ND OF JULY, 1793.

Then, even though Mackay had not yet returned, Mackenzie was ready to begin the return journey. With food supplies virtually non-existent, he could not afford to wait for his lieutenant. Several strange things happened soon after the party left the Dean Channel and reached the muddy flats at the mouth of the Bella Coola River. The tide being very low, the *voyageurs* carried the canoe toward higher ground near the waterfront village. First, the crown prince disappeared ahead on the trail, and a few moments later his warriors hurried off, too. Alexander called to the crown prince. The Indian halted briefly, then raced away again.

Fearing a trick of some sort, Alexander pursued him on foot through the deep, tangled underbrush, leaving the *voyageurs* and Peace River Indians with the canoes and equipment far behind. The crown prince kept about twenty paces ahead of Alexander, he paying no attention now when asked to halt. Then, as they drew near the village, the Indian shouted something unintelligible.

When they emerged from the underbrush and came within sight of the houses, two warriors raced out into the open with daggers in their hands. Both sped toward Alexander, their fierce expressions indicating that they were going to kill him. Instantly dropping his pack, he pointed his rifle at them.

The two braves, understanding the power of firearms, now dropped their daggers. But, though slowing their pace, they continued to advance. Alexander shifted his position and, holding his rifle in his left hand, reached for his cutlass with his right.

Before he could draw it, however, he was surrounded by a large number of warriors who had been hiding in the underbrush. One was the insolent brave who had vowed vengeance for alleged mistreatment at the hands of Vancouver. The natives crowded close to Alexander now, jostling him and rendering useless both his rifle and sword. One of them, managing to sneak behind him, attempted to pin his arms behind his back.

In spite of Alexander's short stature, his physical strength was enormous. He threw the warrior off with such violence that he felt a sharp pain in his left shoulder and thought, for a moment, that he had been stabbed.

Then, using his rifle as a club, he beat his way into the clear, preparing to defend himself against the host, all armed with daggers. His position appeared hopeless. He could kill only one of his foes with the rifle, then would have to reload. As a weapon, his sword was infinitely superior to the daggers of his enemies. Still the odds against him remained tremendous. Nevertheless, bracing himself, he waited for the warriors to leap before firing into their midst.

At that moment, one of the *voyageurs* appeared from the underbrush, carrying a heavy pack. The Indians quickly fled to the shelter of their raised houses.

Soon the rest of the explorers appeared and Alexander told them what had happened. His hat and cloak having disappeared in the scuffle, he said that he intended to take a firm stand here and now. Otherwise the stealing of the expedition's property would continue and the lives of the whole band would be in constant danger.

Rifles were loaded. Then the men formed in a long single line and Alexander solemnly advanced several paces to the front. He fired his pistol into the air; the explosion broke the tense silence. Knowing that the Indians were watching from the houses, he beckoned curtly.

After a long wait, the crown prince climbed down a ladder to the ground. Apologetically he explained that the troublesome warrior had aroused the anger of the village men by accusing the strangers of killing four of his friends. The crown prince, however, offered no explanation for his own peculiar conduct. Alexander let the matter pass for the moment. There were more important issues to be decided.

The murder charges, he declared, were completely false. He had treated all the Indians with kindness as they well knew. Now in return he demanded demonstrations of their friendship. All stolen property must be restored to him at once; in addition, the natives must sell him some fish. In order to emphasize his point, Alexander gestured at his gaunt followers, standing close to him with loaded rifles at their shoulders.

The crown prince hurried back to the nearest house. Soon all the inhabitants except the troublemaker came down to meet Mackenzie. He was given back his hat, cloak, and several knives removed at one time or another from the supply bundles. One of the braves also proffered several small, dried fish. Alexander accepted them in return for a mirror, but demanded additional food.

While these negotiations were in progress, the crown prince suddenly ran to the nearest canoe standing at the river's edge, and, climbing in, he paddled upstream as though pursued by demons.

Alexander made no attempt to follow him, but renewed his request for more fish. The natives, thoroughly cowed, sold him several large, freshly roasted salmon.

Now several poles were obtained from the local Indians. Then the explorers, climbing into the largest of their canoes, began to pole upstream. The current was swift and their baggage was heavy, so they made slow progress. Meanwhile one of the Peace River guides had fallen ill; he sat hunched in his seat, moaning incessantly. Most of the men were suffering from head colds; they seemed about to collapse, too. To make matters worse, when the party paused for a short rest by the river's edge, they saw the trouble-making warrior paddling upstream with several of his friends.

All at once the *voyageurs* became hysterical. Under no circumstances would they go home by way of the river, they shouted. They would find some other route. If necessary, they would crawl on their hands and knees but they would not travel by water. Then, acting as if possessed by evil spirits, they began to throw into the water all their personal belongings except their blankets.

Alexander sat on a rock, listening patiently until their fury was spent. Then he began to reason with them, presenting his arguments logically. He wanted to go home, too, he said, but the fastest and best way was by boat.

The *voyageurs* replied that they would follow him anywhere, but they would not sit in a canoe. Alexander calmly ordered them to march along the bank. Then, bundling the sick Peace River guide into the canoe, he himself poled and paddled upstream. Since he moved at a slow crawl, the land party was often forced to stop and wait for him. Eventually, he hoped, the men would come to their senses.

Alexander Mackenzie had never shown a greater instinct for leadership. He was prepared to paddle alone all the way to the Great Divide if necessary. And he was equally ready to fight any hostile Indians. He never rebuked his men for their insubordination. Instead, he secured food for them, indicating repeatedly that he would welcome their return to the canoe. He was tireless, uncomplaining, and utterly without fear.

At every house on the inhabited banks of the river, he paused, exchanged greetings with the local Indians, and bartered goods for salmon and berries, and by nightfall when he was completely exhausted, the boat was loaded with enough provisions to last for at least a week.

The next morning, meeting a group of friendly mainland Indians, Alexander engaged two warriors to help paddle the canoe. These men were industrious; they knew the river so well that they made good progress in spite of the strong current. At last Alexander himself was able to rest, and the *voyageurs* began to feel thoroughly ashamed of themselves.

Their basic attitude had not changed, however. They still insisted they preferred walking all the way to the Peace River fort to riding on turbulent rivers in frail boats. Alexander wisely made no attempt to press them at this time.

That day the party reached the Great Village. Although scores of Indians came down to the shore, neither the old chief, the crown prince, nor any of the chief's other sons were on hand. Alexander sniffed something strange in the air.

The *voyageurs* did not agree with their leader. Male natives were fishing above and below the salmon trap, women were spinning cedar flax and cleaning fish, children were playing in the dusty square that stood in the center of the village. Everything seemed perfectly normal to the *voyageurs*.

Alexander, however, was determined to take no chances. When the inhabitants pressed forward to greet him, he waved them back. Then, drawing a fine in the dirt with the toe of his boot, he indicated that the natives would cross it at their peril. He ordered his men to stand with loaded rifles, ready for any emergency. As the natives watched in wide-eyed silence, he loaded two pistols.

He told the members of his party that he intended to go alone to the house of the old chief. If the Indians seemed about to harm him, he said, he would fire a pistol as a warning. Then his party was to flee by whatever means possible.

Taking the greatest risk he had assumed at any time on the entire expedition, he walked unattended across the compound. Here and there squaws smiled and waved to him; he returned their greetings in stony-faced silence. Tension mounted steadily; a few warriors appeared from behind houses and then hurried away. Their sudden disappearance confirmed Alexander's suspicions that a rough reception was awaiting him.

As he passed by, an old woman, making a paste of salmon roes, berries, and sorrel, held out the bowl of food to him. Though hungry, Alexander did not dare to pause. For the first time, however, his cold, hard expression changed for an instant, and he smiled at the squaw before going on to the dwelling of the chief.

When he came to this house he halted beside the pillars and called. After a long wait, the old chief appeared above and climbed slowly down a ladder to the ground. The crown prince followed him. The chief seemed disturbed; he was scowling darkly and did not speak.

Alexander waited silently, uncertain what to expect. Suddenly the old Indian threw a small object on the ground at his feet, turned, and stalked away.

Alexander recognized a beaded-leather tobacco pouch belonging to Mackay. Instantly he understood the situation. All the Indians of the region must have heard that the strangers would deal severely with anyone stealing their property. The crown prince had confessed that he was a petty thief; the chief, ashamed and grieving, had returned the article. The loss of dignity, plus fear that the crown prince would be killed by the foreigners' fire sticks, were responsible for the old man's gloom.

Calling out to him, Alexander followed and shook his hand. The chief had cut off his hair and blackened his face with soot to show that he had gone into mourning. But Alexander's assurances of friendship restored his equilibrium. They embraced. Then Alexander exchanged embraces as well with the crown prince for whom privately he felt great contempt.

In the reconciliation that followed, the old chief revealed that his sickly youngest son had died. And everyone had feared that the crown prince, too, had been killed by the bellicose tribesmen living nearer to the coast. Alexander sympathized with the chief because the old man had been living under a severe strain. But, even though good relations had been re-established, Alexander and his men kept their loaded pistols and rifles handy as they ate.

Gifts were exchanged the next morning before the explorers started out on the trail. The *voyageurs* now faced an unusual problem. They carried more food than they could eat, but roasted salmon would spoil in a day or two and so would raspberries. Therefore, while there was plenty for the moment, the long-range prospects remained bleak. The sale of fish still depended on the caprice of local chiefs and game was still scarce.

But the spirits of the *voyageurs* had improved. As they made their way down a forest trail, the men sang of home. The leader refrained from reminding them that danger and privation still lay ahead.

XIX: THE LAST MARCH

THE RETURN TO CIVILIZATION from the shores of the Pacific was a complicated undertaking. The members of Alexander Mackenzie's party knew they could subsist on fish and berries until they reached the plains of British Columbia and Alberta if the natives proved willing to sell them food when their supplies were exhausted. However, this prospect was dubious if recent experience was any criterion. Common sense therefore dictated that the company travel by the shortest route to the Continental Divide and the game-laden prairies beyond the Rocky Mountains.

But Alexander realized that, if he marched too quickly, Mackay might not catch up with him. And if the lieutenant had found Vancouver, the entire band would then be forced to retrace its steps to the coast.

Taking every factor into consideration, Alexander decided to travel slowly through the vast forest east of the Great Village. On his westward journey he had made a detour around the forest, but now, by blazing his own trail through it, he hoped to accomplish several results at the same time: he would be marching in a direct line, so there would be fewer miles to cover; he would take his time and give Mackay a chance to join him; above all, he hoped to find elk, deer, and caribou in the forest — he refused to believe the local Indians who said there was no game in the wilderness, particularly now in the middle of summer.

The trees here were the largest the easterners had ever seen. Many cedars stood twenty-four feet around. And the stately alders, with a circumference of seven feet, were at least three times as thick as alders found east of the Great Divide.

A barking noise attracted the attention of the man. Soon they saw a puppy they had adopted on their westward journey. The animal had wandered away in the woods and had not been found. Now it had grown so painfully thin that the explorers scarcely recognized it at first. But the puppy knew them, racing to one or another of the men, then dashing away again. Obviously the animal was both hungry and frightened.

Alexander halted, opened his pack, and threw the puppy a chunk of salmon. After the *voyageurs* followed his example, the animal quickly became tame again. From that moment until the end of the journey, it was a permanent member of the party. For many years afterward it remained Alexander's devoted pet.

The night was spent deep in the wilderness. Because the explorers still distrusted the intentions of the Great Village inhabitants, no fire was lighted. The company ate cold fish and berries. At Alexander's instigation, the men left the path, carefully covering their tracks, and made themselves as comfortable as possible in the prickly underbrush. No one stood guard duty; instead, each man was made responsible for his own safety. The puppy curled up beside Alexander; both spent a quiet night.

Early in the morning, while the men were again eating a breakfast of cold salmon and raspberries, approaching footsteps could be heard. Loaded rifles were pointed toward the trail; Alexander silenced the growling dog. Soon the figures of four men could be seen. Alexander, recognizing Mackay's party, shouted joyfully and threw down his rifle.

The entire company being now reunited, the morning's march was begun at once. Mackay made his negative report about Vancouver as they walked through the forest. The *voyageurs* then knew they must rely on their own efforts if they hoped to reach home safely.

Additional food was obtained from the Salish now; Alexander marked their community on his map as the Friendly Village. Food still was the most pressing of problems, however. Each man was made responsible for his own rations, the provisions being divided into equal shares. Each of the explorers received about twenty pounds of roasted salmon and five pounds of native "cakes" made of salmon roes, sorrel, and berries. In addition, each was given a small quantity of pemmican, several handfuls of parched corn and a few of corn flour. Alexander kept in his own pack, for emergency use, a quantity of edible hemlock-rind, a Salish delicacy.

When the party emerged from the forest, they began to climb the foothills of the rugged chain of coastal mountains. Marching up slopes that had been so easy to descend tried the endurance of the weary travelers. The convalescing Peace River guide was so tired that Alexander volunteered to carry his pack. Stronger men frequently stumbled and, sitting on the ground, wept in frustration.

On the first night in the mountains, Alexander stayed awake. Sitting with the puppy nestling close beside him, he enjoyed the awe-inspiring view. The precipice they had climbed was so steep that he could look almost straight down to the valley below. Ahead rose magnificent snow-covered mountains. It was odd, he reflected, how much the seasons had changed in only a few hours. Down in the valley, grass was deep, berries were ripe, and trees were in full leaf. Here he could see patches of snow; the ground was still bound by frost, and grass was just beginning to grow. The first blossoms were starting to appear on crowberry bushes. The party had enjoyed summer in the valley; here on the heights it was spring.

The weather was good. Days were sunny, nights clear. Mosquitoes and flies had disappeared, and there were no signs of Indians anywhere. All the natives of the immediate area, Alexander speculated, must have gone west for salmon fishing. On Sunday, July 28, the explorers reached the spot where they had buried their last reserves of pemmican. The food had not been touched. That night everyone ate heartily. The shoulder packs were now only half as heavy as those the men had carried westward, and the party's spirits continued to rise. A long portage through the wilderness, the *voyageurs* decided, only helped to stretch the muscles of strong men. Once again they raised their voices in song.

At two o'clock in the afternoon of August 4, the company arrived at the place near the Fraser River where the canoe, heavy equipment, and major supplies of food had been hidden. Alexander realized that precisely one month had passed since they had left that spot for the Pacific.

Neither provisions nor equipment had been touched; the canoe also was in perfect condition. The occasion called for a celebration. After a huge fire was built, the men cooked flat pancakes of corn flour and distributed large portions of pemmican. Alexander then opened a keg of rum. He gave every man a dram and, at the urging of the whole company, took one himself. Liquor had never meant anything to him, so he was not surprised to find that he did not enjoy his drink. But the *voyageurs* were astonished to discover that, after not having tasted alcoholic beverages for a month, rum no longer appealed to them in the slightest.

The blazing campfire attracted the attention of the local natives. When the explorers emerged from their tents the following morning, several parties of warriors, squaws, and children were approaching. Alexander rewarded them for the care they had taken of his property; he distributed gifts of cloth, steel knives and mirrors.

Then he dispatched Mackay and the *voyageurs* to recover the caches of pemmican buried here and there on the banks of the Fraser. The *voyageurs*, showing none of their previous sulkiness, eagerly took their places in the canoe and sang lustily as they paddled.

While Mackay's party was gone, Alexander became once again a man of business. Producing now all the large knives he had brought on the journey, he traded them for large bales of prime beaver. The trip, he estimated, would be financially profitable. The sale of the furs would more than cover the money spent on wages, equipment, and supplies. Eventually his Montreal partners would receive an explicit account of his transactions.

On the morning of August 5, while all his own men except Bishop were still off collecting hidden packs of pemmican, Alexander discovered that the Indians had stolen most of his baggage. Cooking pots and bags of gunpowder, fishing nets and even spare sleeping bags had vanished. The mentality of these people puzzled him. They had touched nothing during the party's absence. Now that the explorers had returned, however, everything they owned was considered fair game.

But the pragmatic Alexander wasted no time on imponderables. His one concern was the recovery of his property. Because he and Bishop were outnumbered by scores of warriors, even the threat of force would achieve nothing except to arouse the guilty braves' anger. So Mackenzie made use now of what he had learned about the taboos and superstitions of the valley tribes.

Summoning all the natives remaining in the area, he asked whether it was true that they, like the people further to the west, made salmon the mainstay of their diet. Yes, indeed, they said. Their very living depended upon the "fish with pink flesh" that came each year to the waters of the Fraser.

Did they know, Alexander persisted, that these fish made their permanent home in the great sea of foul-tasting water to the west? Most of the natives had visited the coast; they agreed Mackenzie was right.

Had they heard, he demanded, his voice rising wrathfully, that the great sea belonged to men like himself who sailed up and down the coast in huge wooden canoes?

There was absolute silence.

Since the salmon came from the sea, Alexander went on, they belonged to his people. Therefore, if the many articles that had been stolen from his camp were not returned immediately, he would order the gods of the salmon to direct the fish into other rivers. The natives of the highlands would then starve to death.

His logic made complete sense to the Indians; it matched all their religious beliefs.

The battered iron pot in which most of the explorers' meals were cooked now suddenly appeared from nowhere. Two of the three missing bags of gunpowder were deposited in front of Alexander's tent. Two warriors brought him a box of bullets that he had not even missed. Others came with axes and knives, sleeping blankets and fishing nets. But he still was not satisfied.

Again calling together all the natives, he told them to send word to relatives and friends who had already left for their homes. Everything stolen must be returned before sundown or the gods of the salmon would revenge the thefts.

Runners were dispatched. Braves set out in canoes to dash up and down the Fraser, carrying the stern word of this powerful foreigner. Soon whole families reappeared at the bivouac, bringing with them all they had pilfered. Alexander received each brave in turn and accepted the stolen goods. Then, thanking the warriors, he assured them that he forgave them freely and promised that no harm would come to their squaws and children. By late afternoon, all the stolen property had been recovered and the natives had departed.

Mackay and the *voyageurs* returned in the canoe at sundown, bringing with them all the pemmican; it had not been touched. After everyone enjoyed a long night's sleep, the journey was resumed at dawn on August 6. Equipment and supplies had been reduced so drastically that the whole company of eleven men could now ride comfortably in the canoe. The *voyageurs* were pleased, even though poling and paddling upstream against a strong current was, as usual, a difficult task.

Later that day Alexander saw a fascinating sight. Thousands of salmon were swimming upstream, fighting the current. The water boiled, and the schools of fish were so enormous that the surface of the river, as far as any one could see either upstream or down, appeared to be covered with fins.

The Peace River Indians amused themselves by scooping salmon out of the river with their bare hands. Soon the entire party was participating in this sport; dozens of fish were hauled into the boat with no effort. That night the men gorged on roasted and fried salmon; they cooked enough to last for several more days as well.

Salmon still filled the Fraser from bank to bank when the canoe was launched the next morning. So many fish were caught that day and the next that the *voyageurs* and Peace River Indians grew tired of the taste. Indeed, the mere odor of salmon offended them.

Suddenly the pink fish disappeared. They vanished overnight so completely that the two native guides from the Peace River wondered uneasily whether the myths and taboos of the western Indians had come true. Alexander himself made no attempt to analyze the mystery. He merely reported the incident in full for the scientists of the world's great universities.

The swampy portage that had caused so much misery on the westward journey was negotiated again and with difficulty. The weather was cold with a hint in the air of autumn. The men stumbled frequently, often risking their lives in the half-frozen bog. No one complained, though, for each heavy, faltering step brought the company closer to home.

On August 16 the party recrossed the Great Divide and Alexander fell ill. For two days his ankles had been swelling; he was now so lame that, in spite of his protests, Mackay ordered him carried by four men in an improvised litter. After that, his condition began to improve almost immediately.

The canoe was launched again and because the boat was traveling with the eastward flowing current, the pace increased. The *voyageurs* and guides became jubilant when they caught large numbers of whitefish; they were heartily sick of salmon and told Alexander that even the puppy preferred whitefish.

The water level in the canyon of the Peace River had dropped fifteen feet since the westward journey, but Alexander still took no chances. A portage was made. The men were now traveling through the hills and into the prairie at the best possible time of year. The sun overhead was hot, but cool breezes blew down from the mountains. The swarms of mosquitoes and other insects had vanished. Game was found everywhere — elk in the hills and buffalo on the prairie. Everyone gorged on steak.

The habits of civilization were resumed. Soft soap was made from buffalo fat, clothes were scrubbed, and the men bathed daily. They shaved every morning, too, taking pride once again in their appearance.

The company was traveling at a leisurely pace. Everyone retired early, slept late, and ate frequently. Gradually the health of the adventurers was restored. Even the puppy became so frisky that a leash of *watape* was needed, to prevent him from jumping out of the canoe into the river. After that he sat in the prow, growling whenever he saw herds of buffalo on the plains.

The current was still swift enough to carry the canoe downstream swiftly and easily. Excitement began to mount. On September 3, a longer halt than usual was made. Threadbare clothing was washed, then spread out on the river bank to dry. The men shaved and bathed with great care; then, taking the rest of the vermilion, they daubed the canoe with paint.

The following day the oarsmen made good time. At noon no one felt hungry, so no stop was made for a meal. At last, as the canoe rounded a point, the stockade was seen in the distance.

The whole company cheered lustily, even the dog barked loudly. The mast was raised and a flag hoisted. Firearms were discharged; the fort's caretakers came down to the water's edge, blinking in amazement. The *voyageurs* paddled furiously now, and at four o'clock in the afternoon of September 4, the party leaped ashore at the place from which they had set out on May 9.

The incredible journey had come to a successful end.

AFTERMATH

ALEXANDER MACKENZIE'S YEARNING for adventure was satiated. He decided to become once again a businessman and a trader. He and all of the men who had reached the Pacific soon went on to Fort Chipewyan. There they received a thunderous welcome. Word of the exploit was dispatched at once to Montreal by way of Grand Portage, and his men were sent to the stockade for the winter.

The two Peace River Indians, finding even as remote an outpost as Fort Chipewyan too confining, departed for their own homes, laden with rifles, ammunition and gunpowder, axes and blankets. They promised to return the following year for their share of the prize money, but they never appeared to collect it. Instead, they became leaders in their own tribe.

The restless *voyageurs* made the long journey to Grand Portage early in the winter and eventually went on to Montreal. When they received their share of the reward the next year, they enjoyed a brief moment of glory. But most of them quickly spent the money and disappeared. Some, if not all, returned to their regular trades. Nothing more is known of them.

Mackay and Bishop traveled east, too, both to take an active part in the affairs of the North-West Company. Since their knowledge of the Pacific northwest was valuable, Simon McTavish put them to work at once. They carried with them the many notes that Alexander had written to his partners, and now made good use of them in the frantic preparations of North-West to expand its trade.

Alexander remained at Fort Chipewyan through the entire winter of 1793-94. He arose early each day, spending long hours expanding and refining the many hundreds of pages of notes written on his journey. Roderic suggested he should write a book about his exploits, but Alexander did not believe that anyone except fur-traders or college professors would be interested in his adventures. His cousin kept nagging him, however, so he finally consented. In the latter part of the winter he began work on what would eventually become *Voyages from Montreal through the Continent of North America to the Frozen and Pacific Oceans in 1789 and 1793.*

On long, cold winter evenings he discussed the future with Roderic. Although tempted to organize another expedition to find the headwaters of the Columbia River, he wisely decided to terminate his life of adventure. At the age of thirty, he concluded he was becoming too old for the hardships of the wilderness. Although still in good health, he realized that death or serious injury might await him if he persisted in living recklessly. Even before leaving Fort Chipewyan, he knew that he would be hailed throughout the civilized world for his achievements. He was content now to rest on his laurels.

Realizing that he might not visit the northwest again, he lingered at the fort until late in the spring of 1794. Frequently he went out into the open for long, solitary walks. He also enjoyed supervising the flourishing trade with the Indians. On at least three occasions he made short trips into the wilderness, distributing gifts to the natives and encouraging them to sell furs to North-West.

Roderic, having fallen in love with the northwest country, decided to remain at Chipewyan as the partner in charge of that vast territory. He was destined to spend most of his life in the area, although he made many trips to Montreal and in later years occasionally visited England and Scotland. The Canadian wilderness, however, remained his primary interest. He organized the expeditions that traveled across the Rocky Mountains to the Pacific, and became the most important of North-West's active partners in the field.

Alexander finally left Fort Chipewyan in late May, 1794. Traveling by easy stages, he made the long journey to Grand Portage. No one cheered when he walked through the compound. *Voyageurs* and Indians just stood silently, staring at him in open-mouthed wonder. Clerks greeted him so respectfully that he felt uncomfortable. Even the three or four local North-West partners were awe-stricken.

Montreal was stunned, too, when he reached the city in August. Everyone knew him, thousands paid him homage. As he walked through the streets, men doffed their hats to him, women curtsied. Every word he spoke in public was repeated by citizens anxious to boast of his acquaintance.

His reception now in the North-West board room in no way resembled the welcome he had received there after his Arctic journey. No one dared to argue with him now; even Simon McTavish listened carefully when the discoverer of the northwest passage expressed his views.

The partners, under Alexander's direction, made careful plans to expand their trade and tap the virtually unlimited potential of the territory west of the Great Divide. Alexander renewed his plea for a merger with the Hudson's Bay Company. The shortest route to the Pacific, he declared, was through the area controlled by Hudson's Bay. A merger, therefore, seemed inevitable.

His partners, anxious to keep their wealth rather than share it with their rivals, balked at the suggestion. Nevertheless, negotiations were opened. These dragged so interminably, however, that the union of North-West and Hudson's Bay was not actually consummated until several years after Alexander's death. Throughout most of his life, he continued to press for the merger and eventually made the directors of both companies realize that their mutual best interests would be served by joining hands.

Prince Edward Augustus, the fourth son of King George III and a distinguished soldier later to become a field marshal and the Duke of Kent, was in Canada at the time of Alexander's arrival in Montreal. He was anxious to meet the renowned explorer. The wealthy young prince and the little Scotsman who had grown up in dire poverty soon discovered they were kindred spirits; their friendship lasted until the end of their days.

Simon McTavish could not do enough now for his distinguished young colleague. At his instigation, Alexander was made a member of the Beaver Club in Montreal, an exclusive organization all of whose members had spent at least twenty-five years in the fur trade. Alexander took up residence at the club and thereafter it became his Canadian home.

Late in 1794, he sailed to England. In a formal court ceremony he was presented to the King with Prince Edward Augustus acting as his sponsor. Alexander also became friendly with the Prince of Wales, later the Prince Regent and eventually George IV. That winter and spring Alexander was the most popular man in London. No social event was considered a success unless he attended it; he received scores of invitations to dinners and parties every week.

He rejected nearly all of them, for a gay social life did not appeal to him. Etiquette did not permit him to turn down invitations from the Prince of Wales, however, so he was seen frequently in royal circles. His friendship with Edward

Augustus grew as well, and the two men often traveled together. Londoners shook their heads in wonder when the pair kept spending a week or two at a time with troops in the field, sleeping in tents and living on simple foods.

In 1795, Alexander returned to Canada. Making his headquarters at Montreal, he worked furiously for the next six years. His partners in the North-West Company, recognizing him as the equal of Simon McTavish, placed him in charge of supervising all the trade in the great new areas he had opened up. Amassing a great fortune, he was rightly considered one of Canada's wealthiest men.

Personal habits formed earlier in his life remained unchanged. Although forced to attend many banquets, he refused rich sauces or fattening desserts, saying they did not agree with him. He always slept with a board under his mattress in his simple bachelor's quarters at the Beaver Club. Frequently he made day-long trips to North-West's warehouses at nearby Lachine, where he enjoyed sitting down to a meal of unsalted whitefish, venison, and buffalo with any *voyageurs* who happened to be present.

During this period, Mackay, now in comfortable financial circumstances, left the North-West Company to strike out on his own. "Wilderness fever" continued to grip the second-in-command of the journey to the Pacific; he took part in several expeditions to the west. In 1805, he became a partner in a group that planned to sail up and down the Pacific coast, trading with the natives. The members of this expedition were attacked by warriors, and Mackay himself was clubbed to death.

Bishop enjoyed better fortune. After making a number of trips to the northwest, he was promoted in the last years of the eighteenth century to the rank of *bourgeois*, and became one of

North-West's London agents. He settled down in England, marrying an English girl. Twice, in later years, he and his family visited relatives in New Haven.

Alexander Mackenzie returned to London in 1801. Prodded by Roderic, he had continued to work on his *Voyages*. He arrived in England a short time before his book was published. It created an overnight sensation; the publisher could not print enough copies to keep up with the demand.

A German translation, appearing the following year, was equally successful. In France, then engaged in a bitter war with Great Britain, a publisher calmly produced a pirated edition of the *Voyages*. This edition came to the attention of Napoleon himself; he read it with enormous relish.

Out of Napoleon's interest grew a wild and impractical scheme. France, so Napoleon proposed, would send an army to the Pacific northwest with Marshal Carl Bernadotte in command. This expedition would march east through the wilderness, take the Canadians by surprise and capture the country. In time even Napoleon admitted that the idea was far-fetched; the venture was abandoned.

Alexander remained in London for the better part of a year. There, much to his surprise, he was knighted in 1802. Apparently he was the only man in England who did not know he was going to receive the honor.

Late in the same year Sir Alexander Mackenzie returned once more to Montreal. His prestige was now so great that Simon McTavish voluntarily retired from the chairmanship of North-West, Sir Alexander taking his place. In the next six years, the company prospered as never before. The American expedition of Lewis and Clark had found another passage overland to the Pacific, but Alexander was determined not to lose the bulk of the fur trade to the United States. He subjected his partners and the senior clerks to such great pressure that several privately complained, saying that he drove them as mercilessly as he had driven his *voyageurs* on his journeys of exploration.

By 1808, Alexander had grown tired of the world of business. He was so wealthy that money had little meaning any more. He then spent a brief period in politics, representing the county of Huntingdon in the Parliament of Lower Canada, but he was soon bored. He found the speeches of others dull, nor did he enjoy speaking himself. Alexander Mackenzie had always been a man of action, preferring deeds to words.

He retired to Scotland, bought a large farm, and took great joy in managing the property himself. In 1812 and for the first time in his life, he developed a romantic interest, falling in love with a namesake, Geddis Mackenzie of the little town of Avoch. They were married late in that same year; their union was completely successful. They continued to live on the farm.

Alexander remained a major shareholder in North-West, but his desire for a merger with the Hudson's Bay Company waned. A new generation had risen to power, and the directors of Hudson's Bay were trying to bring settlers to the northwest in large numbers. Alexander opposed the project, wanting to keep his beloved wilderness in a wild state.

On March 20, 1820, Alexander Mackenzie died suddenly of a heart attack at the age of fifty-seven. The physical hardships endured on his journeys of exploration and the pressures to which he had subjected himself had taken their toll. All Canada mourned his passing, as indeed did Scotland and England.

Ironically, in 1821 the North-West Company and the Hudson's Bay Company finally merged. And in the years that followed, the vast wilderness that Alexander had loved so well rapidly became civilized.

SELECTED BIBLIOGRAPHY

Mackenzie, Sir Alexander. *Voyages from Montreal through the Continent of North America and to the Frozen and Pacific Oceans in 1789 and 1793*: London, 1801.

———. *Journals*: London, 1814, 1817, 1822.

Brebner, John B. *The Explorers of North America, 1492-1806*: A. & C. Black, London, 1931.

Chambers, E. J. *The Great Mackenzie Basin*: Kings Printer, Ottawa, 1908.

Cook, James. *Voyages to the Pacific Ocean*: London, 1784.

Davidson, Gordon C. *The North-West Company*: University of California Press, Berkeley, 1918.

Innis, Harold A. *Peter Pond, Fur Trader and Adventurer*: Irwin and Gordon, Toronto, 1930.

Mackenzie's Rock, Historic Sites Series, No. 6: Dominion National Parks Branch, Ottawa, 1925.

Manuscript Journals of Alexander Henry and David Thompson, 1799-1814: London, 1826.

Mirsky, Jeannette. *The Westward Crossings*: Allen Wingate, London, 1951.

Morton, Arthur S. *A History of the Canadian West to 1870-71*: Thomas Nelson, London, 1931.

Reed, Charles C. *Masters of the Wilderness*: University of Chicago Press, Chicago, 1914.

The Original Journals of Lewis and Clark, ed. by R. G. Thwaites, 7 vols.: Dodd, Mead and Co., New York, 1904-1905.

Thwaites, R. G. *Peter Ponds Journal*: Wisconsin Historical Collection, Madison, 1908.

Woollacott, Arthur P. *Mackenzie and His Voyageurs*. J. M. Dent, London, 1927.

A NOTE TO THE READER

If you have enjoyed this book enough to leave a review on **Amazon** and **Goodreads**, then we would be truly grateful.

The Estate of Noel B. Gerson

SAPERE BOOKS

Sapere Books is an exciting new publisher of
brilliant fiction and popular history.

To find out more about our latest releases and
our monthly bargain books visit our website:
saperebooks.com